PM+

Teachers' Guide

Levels 3–5

Annette Smith and Jenny Giles
Introductory pages by Elsie Nelley

Nelson I(T)P[®]

102 Dodds Street
South Melbourne 3205

Email nelsonitp@nelson.com.au
Website http://www.nelsonitp.com

Nelson I(T)P[®] *an International Thomson Publishing company*

First published in 2000
10 9 8 7 6 5 4 3 2 1
05 04 03 02 01 00

Text copyright © Annette Smith, Jenny Giles and Elsie Nelley 2000
Photographs copyright © Nelson ITP 2000

PM Plus Teachers' Guide: Levels 3–5
ISBN 0 17 009600 9

Cover designed by John Canty
Edited by Jay Dale
Photographs by Margi Moore and Bill Thomas (page 9)
Illustrations by Vaughan Duck
Printed in Australia by Ligare Book Printers

Nelson Australia Pty Limited ACN 058 280 149
(incorporated in Victoria) trading as Nelson ITP.

Contents

What the PMs are about

The books in the PM Plus series have been written to complement the books in the PM Library and to be used alongside them. Like all the other PM titles, every aspect of the PM Plus titles has been carefully thought through and shaped to meet the developmental needs of young children who are learning to read.

The philosophy that underpins all the material in the PMs is based on the teaching and writings of Dame Marie Clay, the pioneering work of Myrtle Simpson and Pat Hattaway at the Department of Education, New Zealand, and Warwick Elley's research on words children use in their writing. The PM authors — Beverley Randell, Annette Smith and Jenny Giles — have brought their extensive, hands-on classroom experience in teaching beginning readers to the writing and final shaping of the books.

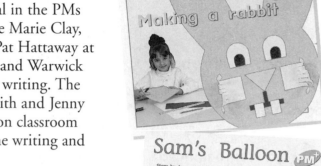

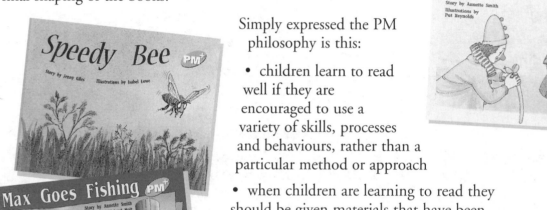

Simply expressed the PM philosophy is this:

- children learn to read well if they are encouraged to use a variety of skills, processes and behaviours, rather than a particular method or approach

- when children are learning to read they should be given materials that have been carefully crafted to meet their needs; books that give them, from their earliest experiences with the printed word, success, enjoyment and understanding.

Every book in the PM series has been shaped to support these twin tenets. On every page in every book care is taken with the sentence structures; the choice of words; the clear, well-spaced type; and with the meaningful, accurate illustrations. Because the books are easy as well as interesting, children are able to practise a variety of reading skills and enjoy the feedback of success.

Each PM Story Book has a classic story structure and deals with concepts and experiences children can understand. It is a real reading experience and has an intrinsic worth because it offers children a proper story structure with tension, climax and resolution. PM Story Books tempt children to reread. They want to revisit the text in order to recapture the success and enjoyment they experienced the first time the stories were read.

Some children prefer reading non-fiction. It fascinates them. In the PM Non-fiction titles the text is carefully researched, accurate and truthful in the way it deals with its subject matter. Clear and logical presentation of the facts, coupled with superb photography and realistic illustrations, make the books relevant, satisfying and enjoyable to read. A delight in truth and a respect for the real world in all its diversity are very much part of the PM meaning-driven philosophy.

All the PM titles have been written using carefully selected vocabulary. In each successive book in the series beyond Level 5, there is a very low ratio of new word introduction (at most 1:20). Each title is completely child-centred and full of meaning. Meaning is paramount in the PMs.

What are the skills, processes and behaviours children use when reading PMs?

The text, illustrations and page layouts of all the books in the PM series have been designed so that children can:

- develop the right concepts about print

- acquire a growing number of high frequency words (sight words)

- build and use a storehouse of known words

- use visual, syntactical and semantic cues to derive meaning from text

- apply reasoning and prediction skills

- link the reading and writing processes

- practise self-extending skills.

When beginning readers are being helped towards literacy, no one skill should be allowed to exclude the other important skills that are needed in the complex and multi-faceted task of learning to read. The PM materials allow children continual opportunities for developing the skills, processes and behaviours to become successful readers.

What is it about the books themselves that give children success, enjoyment and understanding?

1 Because success matters, a very **gentle learning gradient** or **levelling system** has been created. This is so that children are not confused by being asked to process too many unknown words on a page. Each book has been graded to avoid frustration-level reading, the situation in which a child makes so many errors that the meaning of the text is lost. The built-in meticulous levelling of a PM book gives teachers confidence that:

The same high frequency words will be reinforced in several books at the same and succeeding levels.

- new high frequency vocabulary will be introduced slowly
- the same high frequency words will be reinforced in several books at the same and succeeding levels
- text length will be appropriate for the reading experience of the young child
- skills can be introduced when developmentally appropriate
- language structures will match and extend the child's spoken and thinking vocabulary.

2 Illustrations should help children interpret the story and add to their success and understanding. Enormous care and attention is paid to the **close match of text and illustration** in a PM book. Writer's drafts are revised many times, artist's roughs are re-drawn and photographer's shots may be re-taken several times before the authors and publisher consider the books convey the essential meaning to the young child.

The illustration style is most often realistic, so that nuances of meaning and emotion can be portrayed in characters' faces and body language, thereby enhancing and giving depth to the child's understanding of the story.

Realistic illustrations enable characters' emotions to be portrayed.

'The reader needs the kind of text on which the reading behaviour system is working well… at the heart of the learning process there must be the opportunity for the child to use a gradient of difficulty in texts by which he can pull himself up by his bootstraps.'

Becoming Literate: the Construction of Inner Control, *Marie Clay*, Heinemann, 1991.

A specially modified font is used for the earliest books, and there is adequate space between letters, words and lines.

3 A specially modified font is used for
the earliest books, and here the text
itself is carefully positioned on the page to help young children with
directionality. Adequate space between letters, words and lines is provided so
immature eyes can see each letter and word clearly. Each line break and page
break is carefully considered so that it contributes to the meaning of the story.
Each serifed font used at a later level has been selected for its clarity and grace.

Why do children get so much enjoyment from reading PMs?

Proper story structure puts life into the simplest of books.

One of the recurring comments from
teachers using PMs is that a child's first
choice from a selection of books is often a
PM Story Book. One of the reasons is that
they know they will taste success, and that
certainly contributes to their enjoyment.
Without success, enjoyment of reading
is impossible.

Sustained enjoyment comes from the
readable text; the child-centred, high
interest topics; the beautiful
illustrations and the vital ingredient —
a story line. Proper story structure puts
life into the simplest of books by
capturing and holding the reader's
attention. Most children who are
reading a story want to know what will
happen next, so they continue reading
to find out. They can empathise with
the central character(s) and enjoy the
satisfactory resolution on the last page.
Without story structure, beginning
texts become mere reading exercises.

No matter how long or short the story, or how many
variations appear to be woven into it, each PM story follows
the same traditional pattern — the central character(s) has a
problem, and by the end of the book the problem is solved in
a satisfactory way. This structure is detectable, too, in every

quality children's picture book. *The Very Hungry Caterpillar*, *Rosie's Walk*, *Harry the Dirty Dog* and all the timeless favourites such as *Cinderella* or *The Three Billy Goats Gruff* are written in 'story form'.

A story is a powerful way of delivering enjoyment, and always will be… and because stories are powerful they can 'hook' children on to reading.

A variety of lifestyles, families and ethnic groupings is evident in the PM titles.

Enjoyment comes from humour

Many PM titles bring a smile to children's faces with their gentle humour. Yet no character is ever laughed at or 'put down' in a PM story. The aim is to make children feel good about themselves, enhancing their self-esteem.

Enjoyment comes from an attitude of acceptance

The acceptance of all, and the variety of life styles, families and ethnic groupings in PM books allow every child to find a character with whom to identify — Aboriginal, African, Asian, Caucasian, Chinese, Hispanic, Indian, Polynesian, and of course, mixed ethnicity. Some children are shown in a family with two parents, some without a father, some without a mother and some without siblings. The role of grandparents in bringing up children is respected. Children with disabilities are shown winning some of life's battles. The portrayal of a balanced community is not contrived; it simply reflects the real world to which children belong, and so adds to everyone's understanding and enjoyment.

Photo Time

Jack's Birthday

Enjoyment grows when characters are loved — in all good literature characters are true to themselves

Many of the characters in the PMs appear in a number of books and their personal character traits are consistently portrayed in each. Children identify with particular characters and seek out stories at later levels about their favourites. Most of the stories are about real children and real-life events. They have a 'ring of truth' that everyone can identify with and enjoy.

Billy is Hiding

A very wide range of topics and genre helps to 'hook' more children into enjoyable reading

The topics covered in the PM books range from the familiar losing of a first tooth, having a birthday, going to school, winning a race, and teasing Dad. There are stories about familiar and unfamiliar animals, animated vehicles, dinosaurs and folk tales. Over 700 different titles cover fantasy, history, natural history, fiction, traditional tales, technology, verse, songs and plays. Children approach reading from many different angles. A wide variety of subject and genre provides a range of choices. This helps teachers to make the right match of book and child.

Reading for pleasure is the most empowering reading that a child does

Enjoyment is one of the intrinsic rewards of reading and good readers do a great deal of reading for enjoyment (which includes the re-reading of old favourites). They gain pleasure because they are good readers. But it makes them good readers, too... all that extra practice means that they have more and more successful encounters with print, and more exposure to known and almost-known words. When a strategy is applied to an unknown word, the sense of a half-familiar passage gives young learners immediate and helpful feedback. In an easy 'reading-for-pleasure' text the child's mind can grip the main message even while puzzling out a new word or two and attending to visual clues. This ability lies at the heart of reading. Reading involves attending to several things at once, and it is only with easy pleasurable texts that such behaviour falls into place.

Why is understanding so important? What has been done in the PMs to help children understand what they read?

Adults read for pleasure and information, and children's reading should have the same goals. 'Getting the words right' is a pointless excercise if the text has no worthwhile meaning.

When classic story structure is used, meaning takes over because these stories hinge on meaning. To understand the story, children have to experience the tension and anticipate that something is going to happen. A satisfying resolution to the initial problem helps children understand the story in a way that an 'up-in-the-air' ending or a 'twist-in-the-tail' ending never could. **The logic of the story line helps children understand.**

> 'Reading for meaning is paramount'
>
> Developing Life-long Learners, *Margaret Mooney, New Zealand Ministry of Education, 1988.*

A child's understanding of a text is increased by carefully drawn illustrations and well-selected photographs.

The **concepts** in first reading books **must be understood** by the very young if they are to become successful readers. If children struggle with obscure fantasy, or any subject matter that is beyond them, their understanding is lost. Without understanding there can be no self-correction. Obscure topics are excluded from PM Story Books.

Understanding is increased by carefully drawn illustrations and well-selected photographs that illuminate the text and deepen meaning for the viewer in all sorts of ways. **Insights come from viewing as well as reading.**

Understanding comes from scientific accuracy, too. Non-fiction should be as accurate as the author can possibly make it, but fiction, too, should respect accuracy. The animal stories that are included in the PM series are all based on the known behaviour patterns and habits of the animals. Even the bear family stories that are fantasy (signalled by their wearing human clothing) have a base of fact — real bears go fishing, like honey, hibernate and have cubs that climb trees. Much reference and research material are supplied by the authors to the illustrators so that all the books are as accurate as possible in terms of scientific detail, landscape, historical background and modern street signs.

The animal stories that are included in the PM series are all based on the known behaviour patterns and habits of the animals.

Meaning shapes every page, every paragraph, every sentence, every phrase and every choice of word. When a novice reader stumbles on a word or a phrase in the text it should not be because the text is awkward or inaccurate, or that it doesn't make sense. Prediction and self-correction, important reading skills, can only work where the text itself makes good sense. Meaning is embedded in every PM book, fiction and non-fiction.

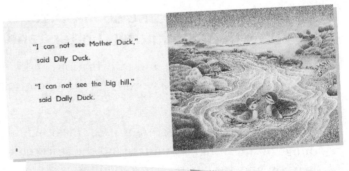

Success, enjoyment and understanding make the task of learning to read worthwhile and help turn young children into self-motivating, self-correcting, self-extending achievers.

With over 700 books in the PM range, teachers have a core reading program for children in their first three years of school — material that will open up children's minds, challenge their thinking and stir their emotions.

The reading classroom

'At the beginning of schooling when children enter formal instruction the foundations of all their future interactions with education are being laid.'

Reading Recovery: A Guidebook for Teachers in Training, *Marie Clay, Heinemann, 1993.*

First teaching practice

Important guidelines for good first teaching practice include:

- early reading experiences where children's responses are accepted as important and worthwhile

- flexible approaches to learning that recognise individual differences

- sensitive observation and analysis of children's language, reading strategies, attitudes and interests

- precise knowledge and understanding of the reading process

- secure relationships between children, care-givers and teachers

- high expectations of the learner

- recognition and extension of the skills and language that children bring to school

- consideration and knowledge of children's home cultures

- access to quality resources.

An effective learning environment

An effective classroom environment encourages children to become involved in learning. The essential features of such a learning environment include:

- appropriate routines and programs that are learner-centred

- an emotionally secure climate

- a curriculum with high expectations for all learners

- programs which cater for children's differing needs and learning styles

- print saturated surroundings where children are immersed in challenging, rewarding language experiences

- opportunities for children to learn and use their developing skills in meaningful ways

- regular feedback that is relevant, appropriate and positive, and where effort is valued

- effective use of classroom fittings and colourful displays

- space for group and class activities

- care-givers who feel comfortable in their interaction with the school.

What is a well-balanced literacy program?

A well-balanced literacy program involves children in reading, writing, listening and speaking. It encompasses a range of experiences and approaches that encourage children to take increasing responsibility for their own learning.

Key elements

Reading to children

Every day the teacher should provide opportunities for children to listen to interesting stories, poems, rhymes and songs. Encourage children to join in. They will gain a love of books and the rhythms of language from experiences with quality literature. When teachers read to children, they provide opportunities for children to experience texts that they are not yet able to read for themselves.

Reading with children

Gradually introduce new challenges to children through shared and guided reading experiences.

Shared book approach

The shared book approach helps children to learn about reading in a non-threatening situation. Usually this involves the whole class, but might also occur with small groups.

While reading with children, the teacher is able to offer support and demonstrate strategies of sampling, predicting, confirming and self-correcting. Shared reading can involve enlarged books, reading charts, songs or poems that are read aloud. Reading to and with children in these ways makes learning pleasurable and children are able to behave like 'real' readers.

Guided reading approach

The guided reading approach supports children in group situations from emergent to fluent reading levels. Small groups are formed because of a common purpose. The teacher guides children as they discuss and read a selected text.

Through guided reading, teachers can assist children to develop positive attitudes and appropriate strategies that lead to independence. During guided reading, teachers provide necessary support while children take increasing responsibility for their own learning.

Reading by children

Have children practise reading with quantities of easy-reading materials. This enjoyable, independent reading activity should happen daily, even at the earliest levels. Children learn to read by reading. Familiar texts lead to children developing an independent self-monitoring system. Children may choose from texts that they have read previously or from texts that the teacher has selected. At other times, they should be able to select personally from a variety of texts — both fiction and non-fiction.

Guided reading

Guided reading is the heart of a well-balanced literacy program for emergent to advanced readers. This approach supports children so that what they do today with the teacher's support, they will be able to do by themselves tomorrow. This is often called 'scaffolding'.

The purposes behind guided reading include:

- support for children as they actively reconstruct meaning by sampling, predicting, checking, confirming and self-correcting

- children experiencing a variety of different texts

- use of carefully selected texts for the teaching and learning of specific skills, reading strategies and fluency

- opportunities for children to become independent, confident readers

- support for children as they discuss, question, read and think their way purposefully through a text

- manageable challenges that encourage children to take increasing responsibility for their own reading of a text

- assessment of children's learning.

> *'The end point of early instruction has been reached when children have a self-improving system.'*
>
> Reading: The Patterning of Complex Behaviour, *Marie Clay, Heinemann, 1979.*

Guided reading leads children to become effective silent readers.

Guided reading enables teachers to:

- interact with a small group of children for specific instruction

- help children to read from a range of different texts

- provide successful reading opportunities to extend children's confidence and language

- use materials with sufficient challenges to increase a child's ability to process

- help children develop a self-monitoring system

- support children as they interact co-operatively with other children

- monitor children's progress frequently and provide constructive feedback

- observe children's understanding and reactions to different texts

- plan learning experiences using information from on-going assessments.

Key elements of a guided reading lesson

Before the lesson

Identify the objective that the children will develop during for the lesson, e.g. children will:

- respond to language and meaning in texts

- select and read for enjoyment

- read for information

- develop conventions of print

- use structural and visual cues to gain meaning

- read with fluency and phrasing

- use personal background, knowledge and experience to enhance understanding.

Choose the best texts to meet these objectives, for example:

- select texts with sufficient known words for children to construct meaning; preferably no more than one new word in every 20 running words
- expect children to read instructional texts with 90–95 per cent accuracy
- select texts challenging enough for children to use skills and strategies confidently as they develop a self-extending system
- select from a range of text forms with meaningful content or well-shaped plots
- select from a wide range of subjects
- select texts where the language is natural and easy to read (containing familiar sentence constructions)
- ensure that the texts have attractive, well-drawn illustrations that enable children to gain maximum understanding.

Identify the purposes for the reading, for example:

- to practise one-to-one word matching or another print convention
- to introduce, reinforce or extend skills or strategies
- to enjoy a story by reading for meaning
- to explore a particular type of text (narrative, descriptive, informative, etc.).

The lesson

Creating the atmosphere

This is the 'tuning-in' stage. It is the time when the teacher focuses children's thinking on the content, concepts or information in the text. At this stage, related language or exciting new vocabulary can be discussed, written on the whiteboard or acted out. In this way, new ideas become familiar and children's language is enriched.

Focusing on the text

This is an in-depth study of the text. The teacher directs questions and discussion to enhance meaning, and to meet the purposes of the reading. Children may be asked to read parts of the text, to answer teacher-directed questions or to clarify what has emerged in discussion. The teacher supports children as they use strategies to solve challenges in the text. The teacher may

A perceptive teacher observes the diverse experiences and understandings of children in the group. They ensure that the text is manageable for children to read in approximately five to ten minutes, is within their understanding and presents an appropriate level of challenge.

intervene to show children how to take responsibility for gaining a deeper understanding of the text. As children become more fluent readers, they are able to read longer sections of the text and even whole stories to themselves.

After the lesson

Going beyond the text

In some lessons, the reading of the text is sufficient and requires no further consolidation activities. At other times, teachers may select language enrichment activities to enhance and extend children's experiences and understandings gained during the reading. These activities give children the opportunity to interact verbally and co-operatively in small groups. They will often extend children's thinking beyond the content of the text.

On-going assessment

Regular assessment of children's progress is an essential component of guided reading. The method and type of information collected will enable the teacher to plan

learning experiences that match children's needs. See also 'Assessment', pages 26–33.

Classroom organisation

Guidelines

- The teacher works with a small group of five to eight children.
- The teacher works with a group for ten to fifteen minutes.
- The teacher works with only two groups daily.
- The children usually sit on the floor in a semi-circle in front of the teacher.
- The teacher selects the text carefully and plans how to present it to the children.
- The teacher provides sufficient books for each child to have their own copy.
- The teacher has a whiteboard or chart to enhance visual learning outcomes.
- The groups are usually selected by reading ability, but they may be based on interest or experience.
- The composition of the groups changes as children achieve at different rates.
- The composition of the groups change when different purposes for the guided reading are identified and planned for.

Planning

Selected groups of children may have guided reading three to four times a week when they are at the emergent and early stages of reading. Guided reading may occur less frequently with fluent readers. However, the session should still take no longer than fifteen minutes. Included is an example of a teacher's daily guided reading plan.

Example of a teacher's daily plan

Date: 8th June

Reading to children

Let's Look at Colours (N. Tuxworth, Lorenz Books, 1996)
Pandas in the Mountains (PM Library Gold Level)

Reading with children

Shared text/s: *The bear went over the mountain* (PM Library Readalongs)

Objectives: •To reinforce recognition of high frequency words.
 •To practise self-monitoring strategies.

Responding to the text/s: Independently reading along with cassette tape.

Guided reading

Group: 1

Text: *Balloons* (PM Plus Level 1)

Purpose: •To introduce a language structure not met before: 'Here is a _____.'
 •To consolidate a knowledge of print conventions.
 •To develop a recognition of high frequency words.

Creating the atmosphere:
•Blow up balloons to match the colours in the book or cut balloon shapes from coloured card.
•Write the colour names on card and place them beneath each balloon.
•Help familiarisation and recognition of the seven colour names.

Focus: Refer to *PM Plus Teachers' Guide: Levels 1–2*, p. 50.

Going beyond the text:
•Use BLM 9 (p. 51) to reinforce the high frequency words: Here, is, a.
•Colour and then paste the BLM verse into children's own poetry anthology.

Group: 3

Text: *Baby Panda* (PM Plus Level 5)

Purpose: •To ensure correct directionality on double-page spread.
 •To introduce ? as a punctuation symbol and its name and meaning.
 •To talk about first and last letters of a word.

Creating the atmosphere:
•Show the children photos of pandas in the wild.
•Talk about the panda's thick coat, and black and white markings.

Focus: Refer to *PM Plus Teachers' Guide: Levels 3–5*, p. 78.

Going beyond the text:
•Use BLM 23 (p. 79) and talk about the common sound at the end of 'runs', 'looks' and 'sees'.
•Have the children illustrate each page of the text and paste these onto the six sides of a box.

Groups: 2 and 4

Independent reading tasks. Refer to *PM Plus Teachers' Guide: Levels 3–5*, pp. 22–23.

Targeted children/learning needs:

Group 1: Tim, Abdul — 1-to-1 and direction
Group 3: Maria, Liam — looking at last letters

Assessment:

Dane, Georgia, Maria

Example of a weekly plan

Here is an example of a weekly guided reading plan. The teacher has planned for four different guided reading groups. A weekly plan may be organised around four days. This allows one day for the teacher to plan for a shared reading or an integrated language experience, and for assessment.

Key

GR — Guided reading with teacher   HFW — High frequency words   BLM — Blackline master
T's G L — PM Plus Teachers' Guide Levels   T — Teacher

Groups	Monday	Tuesday	Wednesday	Thursday
1	• Read simple verses (BLMs Levels 1–2). • **GR** *Balloons* T's G L 1–2, p. 52. • Language structure: 'Here', 'is', 'a' (not met before).	• *Balloons* BLM reinforce HFW: 'Here', 'is', 'a'. • Colour and paste BLM verse into own poetry anthology. • Word games.	• **GR** *In our classroom* – refer to T's G L 1–2, p. 44. • Language structure: 'The', 'go', 'here' (not met before). • Draw pictures of items in classroom, T scribe captions.	• *In our classroom* BLM reinforce HFW: 'The', 'go', 'here'. • Colour and paste BLM verse into own poetry anthology. • Alphabet activities.
2	• Crayon and dye 'photo' of self, T scribe: '_____ is here.' • Read own anthologies. • PM Library Readalongs using headphones.	• **GR** *Photo Time*, refer T's G L 3–5, p. 34. • Encourage fluency and phrasing. • Word games.	• Reread *Photo Time* to selves. Illustrate copies of text for wall story. • Alphabet games and activities.	• Children make 'cars' from boxes. • T discuss cars made, scribe captions. • **GR** *Jack and Billy*, refer T's G L 3–5, p. 44.
3	• **GR** *Baby Panda*, refer T's G L 3–5, p. 78. • Check for correct directionality on double-page spread. • Discuss: 'runs', 'looks', 'sees' on BLM 23 (T's G L 3–5). Children complete the task independently.	• Illustrate copies of text from *Baby Panda*. Paste onto sides of box. • Read, sing and dance to *The bear went over the mountain* (PM Library Readalongs).	• Word recognition games. • **GR** *Run, Rabbit, Run!*, refer T's G L 3–5, p. 82. Scan words for endings: rabbits, comes, sees, looks.	• Children read *Run, Rabbit, Run!* with friend. • Make a mural of Rabbit Hill. T write text from book on mural.
4	• Read, sing and dance to *The big ships sail* (PM Library Readalongs). • Make scrapbook about boats. • Word recognition games and reading own anthologies.	• Independent reading. • **GR** *The Leaf Boats*, refer T's G L 6–8, p. 64. • Demonstrate a remote control car. • BLM 16 (T's G L 6–8).	• Follow T's G L 6–8, p. 64 make leaf boats. Sail in small container. • Write and draw about experience. • Read, sing and dance to *The big ships sail* (PM Library Readalongs).	• **GR** Reread *The play* (PM Plus Level 1) • Read *A Crocodile and a Whale*, refer T's G L 6–8, p. 68. • Reinforce cross-checking strategies. • BLM 18 (T's G L 6–8).

Using a PM Plus text

Each double-page spread in the PM Plus teachers' guides provides a teaching plan and accompanying blackline master. The following descriptions relate to the features found in the teaching plan.

Running words

The exact number of words in the book being explored (see page 29).

About the story

This section contains notes about the story content.

Creating the atmosphere

Before reading the book, the teacher needs to focus children's thinking on the content and concepts. Related language or new vocabulary can be discussed.

Focusing on the story — guided reading

This is the stage when the teacher facilitates discussion and guides the readers.

STORY BOOKS LEVEL 4

Running words: 89

Jack's Birthday

About the story

This is the third story in the PM Plus series about Jack and Billy. In this story, Jack receives a new car for his birthday from his mother and father. Billy is envious and the car disappears. Dad comes to the rescue and all is well.

Linking with other PM books

Birthday balloons	PM Library Blue Level
Baby Bear's present	PM Library Blue Level
Down by the station	PM Library Readalongs

Creating the atmosphere

Reread *Photo Time* and *Jack and Billy* (Level 3). Discuss the characters of Jack and Billy. Talk about how children feel when they are opening presents.

Focusing on the story

- **Cover** Children will recognise Jack and Billy from previous books. Talk about the game Jack is playing with his car.
- **Pages 2–7** Discuss the present that Jack has received for his birthday and how young children react to siblings receiving presents. Comment on the fact that Billy is watching Jack.
- **Pages 8–9** Observe this illustration closely. Discuss what both boys are doing.
- **Pages 10–11** Have the children predict what has happened to the car based on the previous illustration and their experiences with younger siblings.
- **Pages 12–16** Discuss how Dad is involved in solving Jack's problem.

Going beyond the story

- Invite the children to talk about their birthdays and presents that they have received. Have them draw or paint their presents and write captions.
- In the classroom, have the children make a garage with blocks. Extend them further by asking them to make a road for the toy vehicles to travel along. Captions can be used to describe the cars in the garage.

The little cars go up here.

Here is the little bus.

Here is the blue truck.

Developing specific skills

- Link the visual pattern and sound of the initial upper-case letters: M — Mum, D — Dad, J — Jack, B — Billy.
- Encourage picture interpretation. Focus on the details that help to predict text.
- Pattern voice intonation to increase meaning.

Using the blackline master

- Demonstrate how to trace over and complete the word 'said'.
- Read the sentences with the children.
- Talk about the details needed when the children draw their own illustration.

62   PM Plus Teachers' Guide: Levels 3–5

Linking with other PM books

Titles from PM Library and PM Plus that link by theme or language structure to the text being explored.

Going beyond the story

Teachers may select from or adapt these language enrichment activities to meet the needs of their class. All have been designed to develop purposeful and stimulating language.

Developing specific skills

These are the focus skills to be taught. They are not intended to be taught in isolation, but rather in the meaningful context of the child's current reading.

Blackline masters

The blackline masters in the PM Plus teachers' guides have real purpose, engaging children in independent activities that increase their skills with language.

Before children begin work on the blackline masters, discuss the sheet with them to ensure they know what they are doing, why they are doing it and how they are to do it.

Independent reading tasks

While the teacher interacts instructionally with small groups for guided reading, other children may be directed to independent reading tasks. At the beginning of the school year, and regularly throughout the year, an effective teacher will develop routines that support independent activities. Hence, children learn to work independently while the teacher supports a group or groups for guided reading. Independent activities should challenge the children's skill development and support their progress in reading and language.

The teacher needs to ensure that children are familiar with the activities and classroom routines before they are expected to practise them independently.

Children should also be encouraged to read with a friend or in a group, as well as by themselves.

Task ideas

Teach the children how to:

- respond to a text already read, e.g. a language enrichment activity or a blackline master

- revisit familiar books (it is recommended that each child has their own box of independent reading texts)

- read 'big books' or shared reading materials

- work at set tasks that reinforce a shared reading text, e.g. by innovating the text, making a group mural, etc.

- read at the listening post
- use transparencies with an overhead projector
- read stories, captions and labels from around the room
- read poems, rhymes and song charts
- read a variety of different texts from the classroom library
- research and record information
- interact with other children in the alphabet corner (i.e. alphabet books, alphabet lotto, activities for matching letters with pictures, making letters from dough, etc.)
- use reading activities, e.g. word lotto, crosswords, matching words onto poem cards, arranging sentences into meaningful sequences, language jigsaws, etc.
- practise and perform plays
- read published personal and class writing.

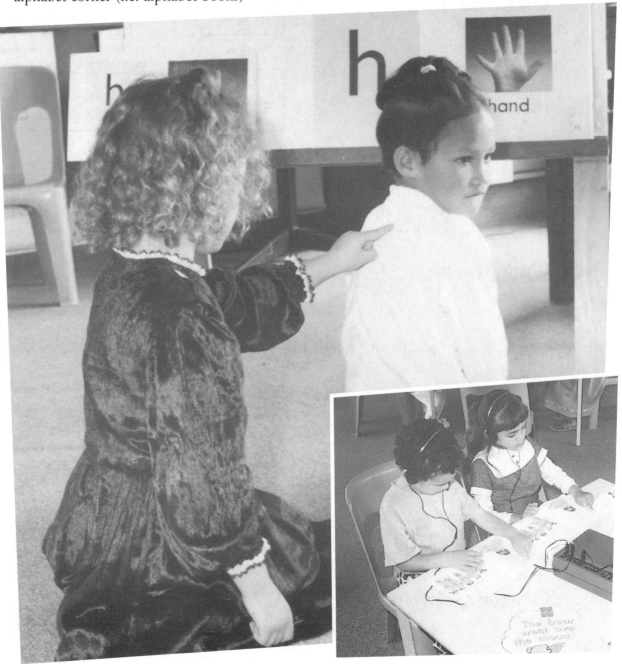

Organising independent reading tasks

Below is an example of a daily program chart organised for independent activities. The teacher makes name cards for groups and/or individual children. These are attached to the chart with Velcro. The teacher moves the cards to direct children to specific activities. Children soon become independent at identifying their daily programs. Allowing children to be responsible for their own program ensures that the teacher is not disturbed while working with a group.

Example of a daily program chart

Guided reading groups	Puppies	Kittens
Responding with directed reading activity	Rabbits	Puppies
Independent reading	Guinea Pigs	Rabbits
Writing centre	Guinea Pigs	Sam / Kerry / Toni / James
Reading activities	Kittens	Guinea Pigs
Big books and poems	Kittens	Guinea Pigs
Listening post /OHPs	Kittens	Guinea Pigs
Computer software	Ki / Lynn / Cody / Jacob	Anna / Ling / Josh / Nilan

Teachers often use picture charts to help children be responsible learners. Here is an example of a classroom chart that helps young children remember the independent reading tasks that they may select.

Example of classroom chart

Assessment

'In complex learning, what is already known provides the learner with a useful context within which to embed new learning.'

An Observation Survey of Early Literacy Achievement, *Marie Clay, Heinemann, 1993.*

Assessment is a necessary component of a successful language program. During assessment, teachers collect information about children's previous learning, language acquisition, skills, understandings, attitudes and interests.

The purpose of assessment is always to improve learning and teaching, i.e. to plan for the child's learning and to improve the program that the teacher implements. Information for assessment should be collected during the daily program.

Assessment procedures

The procedures that the teacher uses to assess reading may include both formal and informal observations, for example:

- anecdotal records of observations
- checklists, e.g. alphabet recognition, high frequency words
- listening to children retell stories
- accurate reading records (see pages 27–32)
- conferencing between the teacher and the child, especially to determine reading for meaning
- self-assessment (children can be taught to set goals).

For a detailed description of taking, scoring and analysing reading records, see An Observation Survey of Early Literacy Achievement, *Marie Clay, Heinemann, 1993.*

Reasons for assessment

The key reasons for assessment are:

- to know the child as an individual
- to identify what the child has already learned
- to identify what needs to be learnt next so that learning experiences match learner needs
- to give the teacher accurate information for organising an effective class program
- to identify the most appropriate approaches and resources for the learner
- to provide constructive feedback to the learner and care-givers
- to monitor progress over time
- to provide information about individual, class or school achievement.

Regular assessment

It is essential for teachers to reflect upon their teaching practices, program outcomes and learning environment. Regular reading assessment identifies:

- how effectively the child is developing a self-monitoring system
- the child's awareness that reading should make sense
- the cues that the child is using or not using
- the child's knowledge of print conventions
- the child's attitudes towards reading
- the child's self perception of himself/herself as a learner
- the child's interests

- the child's abilities with other language skills, i.e. writing, speaking and listening
- the child's rate of learning
- the child's level of independence or requirement for an intervention program
- resource availability and the effectiveness of approaches.

What is a reading record?

At the centre of effective assessment is the technique of taking a reading record. This observation records precisely what the child is saying and doing. It provides an accurate description of the strategies that the child uses when sampling, predicting, checking, confirming and self-correcting.

Many reading records will be taken of the child reading from seen texts. However, unseen texts should be used if the teacher's purpose is to assess the child's confidence and ability to use and integrate strategies independently.

How to take a reading record

Learning to take a reading record takes practice. The child needs to sit or stand beside the teacher. The text must be seen clearly by the teacher and the child. First, ask the child, 'What is this book about?' This 'tunes' the child into the reading. The teacher then records everything that the child says and does while the child reads the text aloud. The teacher does not prompt the child and remains objective throughout the reading.

'The reason for using a "seen" text for the instructional level record is that we want to see how well the reader orchestrates the various kinds of reading behaviours he controls, given that his reading is being guided by the meaningfulness of the text. The "seen" text ensures that the child understands the messages of the text and meaningfulness will guide the reading.'

An Observation Survey of Early Literacy Achievement, *Marie Clay, Heinemann, 1993.*

A reading record should not take more than ten minutes. It is suggested that a reading record should be between 100–150 words (this will be less for texts at the earliest levels). Recording is usually done on a standardised record sheet (see page 111 for a blank 'reading pro forma') or an exact copy of the text (see pages 107–111).

Conventions used for recording

- Mark every word read correctly by the child with a tick.

> ✓ ✓ ✓ ✓
> 3. Here is Kitty Cat.
> ✓ ✓ ✓ ✓
> Kitty Cat is hungry.

- All attempts and errors are recorded by showing the child's responses above the text.

Child:	he	him
Text:	here	

- If the child self-corrects an error, it is recorded as a self-correction, not an error.

Child:	he	SC
Text:	here	

- If a word is left out or there is no response, record it as a dash.

Child:	—
Text:	today

- If a word is inserted, record it.

Child:	✓	✓	✓ always	✓
Text:	Kitty	Cat	is /	hungry

- If the child is told a word by the teacher, record it with a 'T'.

Child:	we	
Text:	where	T

- If the child appeals for a word, the teacher says, 'You try it.' If the child is unable to continue, record 'A' for appeal and tell the child the word.

Child:	we	went	A	
Text:	where			T

- Repetition is not counted as an error, but is shown by an 'R' above the word that is repeated, as well as the number of repetitions, if more than one.

> R or R3
> ✓ ✓
> here here

- Use 'R' for repeats plus an arrow if the child goes back over several words or even back to the beginning of the page.

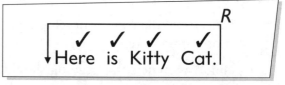

- If the child appears confused, help by saying, 'Try that again.' This is counted as one error only before that piece of text is given a fresh beginning.

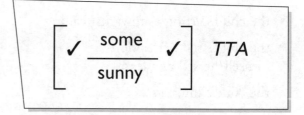

Running words in the PM Library and PM Plus texts

In all PM Plus teachers' guides the number of running words for each text is indicated. Running words for the PM Library and PM Plus follow the rules listed below:

• the words on the cover and title page are not counted

• compound words are counted as one word

• hyphenated words are counted as one word

• animal noises that include a vowel, e.g. 'Baa-baa' are counted as one word

• sounds such as 'sh-sh-sh' are not counted as words

• numbers in numeral form, e.g. 1, 2, 3 are not counted as words, however when they are spelled out, e.g. 'one', 'two', 'three', they are counted.

Scoring a reading record

• The accuracy rate is calculated by dividing the number of words read by the number of errors. Table 1 (see page 30) will assist the teacher to calculate a percentage accuracy score .

• The self-correction rate is calculated by adding both errors and self-corrections together and then dividing by the number of self-corrections.

Analysing reading records

It is essential that the teacher analyses the behaviours that were observed so that the child's next learning step can be planned.

1 The teacher records each error and self-correction in the first two columns of the reading record (see page 32 for an example of a completed reading record). These errors and self-corrections are analysed further on the adjoining columns as:

• 'M' for the meaning

• 'S' for the structure of the sentence

• 'V' for sources of visual information.

2 The teacher analyses the child's behaviour before every miscue. When analysing self-correction behaviours, consider the miscue, then consider what extra information the child used to process the print. If the child has made no attempt to self-correct errors, identify if the child is:

• reading for the precise message, or

• is able to use cues effectively to monitor or problem solve, or

• has control of relevant oral vocabulary to read with understanding.

3 The teacher examines the analysis to determine how the child is responding to the different sources of information in the text.

A cumulative file can be kept of the child's reading progress. Ensure that any reading record kept for filing is dated with day, month and year. Include other forms of assessment such as annotated samples of the child's writing and oral language assessments, as well as reading records. Keep only useful information in organised files.

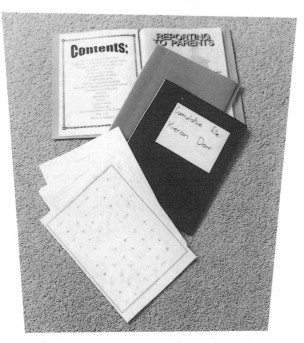

Analysing behaviours

To analyse the reading record, the teacher asks questions about these behaviours:

- Is the child competent with one-to-one matching?
- Does the child have consistent directionality?
- Is the child reading fluently at this level?
- When an unknown word is encountered, does the child:
  - make an attempt
  - make no attempt
  - seek help
  - re-run or repeat the word
  - read on
  - use meaning cues
  - use structural information
  - use visual information?

Table 1

Error rate	Percentage accuracy
1:100	99%
1:50	98%
1:35	97%
1:25	96%
1:20	95%
1:17	94%
1:14	93%
1:12.5	92%
1:11.75	91%
1:10	90%
1:9	89%
1:8	87.5%
1:7	85.5%
1:6	83%
1:5	80%

Scores

An easy text is 96% to 100%.

An instructional text is 90% to 95%. A text that is too difficult is 89% and below.

- When an error is made, does the child:
  - self-correct
  - ignore it
  - seek help
  - re-run or re-read
  - take the initiative to search further?

- When self-correcting, does the child:
  - use meaning cues
  - use structural information
  - use visual information?
- Which accuracy level is the child reading at?

Blackline masters

Reading record sheets

The PM Plus books, with their rich language structures and strong storylines, provide excellent material for monitoring children's control over meaning, language structures and visual information. 'Reading record' examples and a 'Reading record' pro forma (see pages 107–111) have been provided to assist teachers when analysing children's reading competence and skill development. These sheets are reproducible and ideal for the busy classroom teacher. An example of each story book at Levels 3, 4 and 5 has been provided and a non-fiction example has also been included to provide another opportunity for teachers to gauge children's reading skills. Procedures for administering and analysing reading records can be found on pages 27–31 of this book.

Example of a completed reading record

Reading record PM⁺

Name: *James*   Age: *5.4*   Date: *10/5/01*

Text: *Mother Bird*   Level: *4*   Running words: *75*

Summary: *Reruns to search for meaning. Dominant use of meaning and structure. Not yet scanning across work to cross check with visual information.*   *Accuracy 94.5%*   *Self-correction 1:3*

Page		E	SC	Errors MSV	Self corrections MSV
3	✓ ✓ ✓ ✓ ✓ ✓ Mother Bird is looking for a worm.				
5	✓ ✓ ✓ ✓ Up in the tree, birds | sc ✓ ✓ ✓ ↑the baby | birds | are hungry.		1	M S Ⓥ	Ⓜ S V
7	✓ ✓ _looked_ ✓ _looked_ Mother Bird looks and looks	1 1		Ⓜ Ⓢ V Ⓜ Ⓢ V	
	✓ ✓ for a worm.				
9	_is_ | sc ✓ ✓ ↑Here comes | a worm.		1	M Ⓢ V	M Ⓢ Ⓥ
	✓ ✓ ✓ ✓ ✓ Mother Bird sees the worm.				
10	✓ ✓ _the_ ✓ Here comes a cat.	1		Ⓜ Ⓢ V	
	✓ _big_✓ ✓ ✓ The ∧cat sees Mother Bird.	1		Ⓜ Ⓢ V	
13	✓ ✓ ✓ ✓ Mother Bird sees the cat.				
	✓ ✓ ✓ Up goes Mother Bird.				
15	✓ ✓ ✓ ✓ ✓ Up, up, up, goes Mother Bird.				
	✓ ✓ ✓ Mother Bird goes up				
	✓ ✓ ✓ ✓ ✓ ✓ to the baby birds in the tree.				
16	✓ ✓ ✓ ✓ ✓ ✓ The worm is for the baby birds.				
	Totals	4	2	④⑤①	①①①

Language monitoring check

Regular monitoring of children's progress is an essential part of sound teaching practice. A 'Language monitoring check' pro forma (see page 106) has been provided to guide teachers' observations of children's reading and writing behaviours. It will assist teachers to monitor the language skills, understandings and behaviours of speaking, listening, reading, writing, viewing and presenting that should be developing at each stage of language acquisition.

Example of a completed language monitoring check

Language monitoring check PM⁺

Levels 3, 4 and 5
Skills, understandings and behaviours

	James	Luke	Zac	Amy	Brigette	Georgia		Date
Speaking and listening								
Listens to stories	✓	✓	✓	✓	✓	✓		9/5
Tells stories based on own experiences	✓	✓	✓	✓	✓	✓		9/5
Explains about own pictures	✓	✓	•	✓	✓	✓		9/5
Controls a range of appropriate oral vocabulary to suit the situation	✓	✓	•	✓	✓	✓		9/5
Reading and writing								
Has one-to-one correspondence	✓	✓	✓	✓	✓	✓		11/5
Demonstrates correct directional movement with text	✓	✓	✓	✓	✓	✓		11/5
Is linking the text to the meaning	✓	✓	✓	✓	✓	✓		11/5
Has retained many high frequency words	✓	•	•	✓	✓	✓		11/5
Demonstrates front and back of book	✓	✓	✓	✓	✓	✓		12/5
Is developing a memory for text	✓	✓	✓	✓	✓	✓		12/5
Is linking picture clues to text	✓	✓	✓	✓	✓	✓		12/5
Talks to others about own stories and pictures	✓	✓	•	✓	✓	•		12/5
Reads back own stories	✓	•	•	✓	✓	✓		13/5
Is beginning to link sounds to letter symbols	✓	✓	•	✓	✓	✓		13/5
Is attempting unknown words in own reading and writing using the initial letter	✓	✓	•	✓	✓	✓		13/5
Viewing and presenting								
Observes more detail in illustrations	✓	✓	✓	✓	✓	✓		13/5

General comments (date all observations):General comments (date all observations):
· *Monitor Luke and Zac closely in guided and independent reading situations.*
· *Contact parents of these children. Explain how assistance can be given in home.*
· *Establish partner/buddy reading – James/Luke, Amy/Zac, Brigette/Georgia.*
· *Provide more PM Alphabet and Starters books for recreational reading.*

Photo Time

About the story

This book introduces the characters Jack and Billy, and their parents. Jack is five years old and Billy is his younger brother. In this story, the family is trying to persuade Billy to have his photo taken and Jack finds a way of doing this.

Linking with other PM books

Mum	PM Library Starters One
Dad	PM Library Starters One
The photo book	PM Library Red Level

Creating the atmosphere

Read *The photo book* (PM Library Red Level). Invite the children to talk about having their photos taken. Have them bring a photo of themselves with their family to school.

Focusing on the story

- **Cover** Talk about the characters who are introduced in this book and the fact that Jack is the same age as the children in the class.

- **Pages 2–9** Discuss the possible reasons why Billy may not have wanted to have his photo taken.

- **Pages 10–11** Talk about how Jack is trying to encourage Billy to have his photo taken. What kind of photo is he encouraging?

- **Pages 12–13** Discuss why Jack was successful in gaining Billy's attention while Mum and Dad failed. Have the children predict what Billy will do.

- **Pages 14–16** Discuss why Billy went in this photo and not the others.

Going beyond the story

- Make a class book or wall mural using the photos the children brought to school (see 'Creating the atmosphere'). Add captions using vocabulary from *Photo Time*, e.g. 'Sarah is in the photo', 'Sarah's mum and dad are in the photo', 'John and Tom are in the photo', etc.

- Display a class photo. Add captions which feature the children's names.

Developing specific skills

- Focus on the initial upper-case letters of the names as an entry to these words.
- Link the visual pattern and sound of the initial letters: M — Mum, D — Dad, J — Jack, B — Billy.
- Full stop — introduce the punctuation symbol, name and meaning.

Using the blackline master

- Discuss each character's photo. Link their photo to their name.
- Demonstrate how to trace over the names below the photos and in the sentences.
- Have the children draw a picture of each character (head and shoulders only) in the appropriate box.

My name is _____

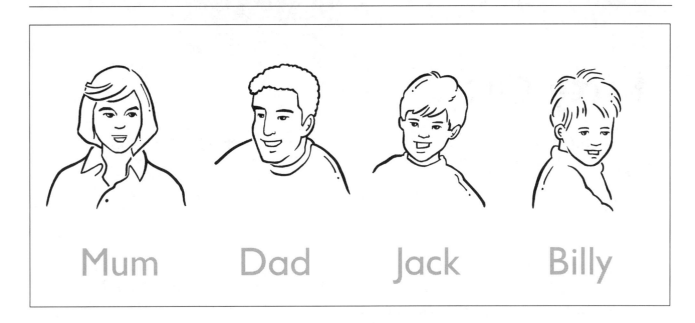

Mum is in the photo.

Dad is in the photo.

Jack is in the photo.

Billy is in the photo.

Blackline master 1 • *Photo Time* © Nelson, 2000.

This page may be photocopied for educational use within the purchasing institution.

PM Plus Teachers' Guide: Levels 3–5   35

Kitty Cat

About the story
This is the first of several stories about a mischievous little cat and an older grumpy cat called Fat Cat.

Linking with other PM books
My little cat   PM Plus Level 2
Pussy and the birds   PM Library Red Level

Creating the atmosphere
Revisit *My little cat* (PM Plus Level 2). Study the photographs and talk about cat behaviour. Discuss how young cats will also chase leaves, and try to catch insects and small animals.

Focusing on the story
- **Cover** Identify Kitty Cat. Talk about her colour and the markings on her fur. Read the title together. Some children may be ready to notice that both the 'k' and the 'c' have the same sound although they are visually different.
- **Pages 2–3** Discuss Kitty Cat's actions and ask what she might be doing. Read the text with the children and help them to decode the word 'hungry' using the initial letter.
- **Pages 4–9** Encourage the use of the illustrations and the initial letter to decode the words 'butterfly' and 'lizard'. Observe the children as they attempt to decode 'hungry', again.

- **Pages 10–11** Talk about Kitty Cat's obvious disappointment. Ask, 'What do you think Kitty Cat will do now?'
- **Pages 12–13** Introduce Fat Cat. Talk about his size in comparison with Kitty Cat's. Read his name on his plate and find it in the text. Predict what Kitty Cat might do next.
- **Pages 14–16** Talk about Fat Cat's actions and Kitty Cat's satisfaction at last.

Going beyond the story
- Draw or paint pictures of Kitty Cat. Encourage the children to copy a sentence from *Kitty Cat* that they feel best describes their picture.
- Role-play some of Kitty Cat's actions. Pretend to creep, pounce, spring, etc.
- Read the children a selection of cat poems. Talk about cat behaviour.
- Make a list of food that Kitty Cat may like to eat. Add illustrations. Remind the children that she is still a young cat.

Developing specific skills
- Link picture and initial letter.
- Full stop — talk about the punctuation symbol, name and meaning.
- Associate the upper- and lower-case initial letter: Hh — Here, here, hungry.

Using the blackline master
- Read each sentence with the word 'Here'.
- Discuss how to trace and write the letters 'Hh' and the word 'Here'.
- Use *h* (PM Library Alphabet Starters) to reinforce the letter and sound.

My name is _____

Here is Kitty Cat.

Here is a butterfly.

Here is a lizard.

Here is Fat Cat.

H   H   ___ ___ ___ ___

h   h   ___ ___ ___ ___

Here   Here   _____ _____

here   here   _____ _____

h

☐ ☐ ☐ ☐

Sam and Bingo

About the story
This book introduces the character, Sam, who lives with her mother and her pet dog, Bingo. Sam makes a farm with blocks for her toys. When Bingo appears, she is at first annoyed, but then incorporates him into her game.

Linking with other PM books
The farm in spring	PM Library Starters Two
My little dog	PM Library Starters Two
Old MacDonald had a farm	PM Library Readalongs
Bingo	PM Library Readalongs

Creating the atmosphere
Read *My little dog* (PM Library Starters Two). Discuss the children's pet dogs and ways in which the children behave and interact with their pets.

Focusing on the story
- **Cover** Talk about the 'farm' Sam has made for her toy animals.

- **Pages 2–5** Discuss the different farm animals that Sam has used and the way she has arranged the fences.

- **Pages 6–7** Have the children predict where the next animal will go.

- **Pages 8–9** Were the children's prediction's correct?

- **Pages 10–11** Encourage the children to predict what Bingo is going to do.

- **Pages 12–13** Ask, 'How is Sam feeling? Why did Bingo come on to the farm?'

- **Pages 14–15** Have the children predict what Sam will do next.

- **Page 16** Discuss Sam's character and her relationship with her dog.

Going beyond the story
- Using *Bingo* (PM Library Readalongs) sing the song and learn the letters of Sam's dog's name.

- Encourage the children to predict a different ending to this story, suggesting other ways that Sam might have reacted, or ways that they themselves might react in a similar situation.

- Make a farm with big blocks and soft toy animals, or plastic blocks and small plastic animals.

Developing specific skills
- Link the visual pattern and sound of the initial upper-case letters: S — Sam, M — Mum, B — Bingo.
- Link the visual pattern and sound of the lower-case initial letters: h — horse, c — cow, p — pig, d — dog.
- Speech marks — introduce the punctuation symbol, name and meaning.

Using the blackline master
- Use *A first alphabet book* (PM Library) page 32 to reinforce the letters S, M, B and h, c, p, d.
- Demonstrate how to trace over 'here' and indicate its position in the sentence.
- Show the children where to draw the farm, the three animals and Bingo.

My name is _____

here here _____ _____

Sam is here.

Bingo is here.

The horse is _____.

The pig is _____.

The cow is _____.

The farm is _____.

Little Chimp

About the story
This book introduces the characters of Little Chimp and Mother Chimp who live in a chimp community in a forest. Mother Chimp returns to Little Chimp when he wakes up and calls to her.

Linking with other PM books
Looking down	PM Library Starters Two
The baby owls	PM Library Red Level
Joey	PM Library Green Level

Creating the atmosphere
Using *Monkeys and Apes* (PM Library Animals Facts Turquoise Level) introduce the children to the illustration of a mother and baby chimp (see page 14). Discuss the environment in which chimpanzees live.

Focusing on the story
• **Cover** Discuss Little Chimp's character and features.

• **Pages 2–3** Talk about how Little Chimp and his mother are sleeping together in their nest made of leaves and branches high up in the tree.

• **Pages 4–9** Discuss what Mother Chimp does while Little Chimp is asleep.

• **Pages 10–11** Talk about how Little Chimp feels when he wakes up and discovers that he is alone. Discuss the relationship between Little Chimp and Mother Chimp, and how young animals are reliant on their parents.

• **Pages 12–13** Predict what Mother Chimp will do when she realises that Little Chimp has woken up.

• **Pages 14–16** Look closely at Little Chimp. Compare how he was feeling when he was alone with how he feels now that his mother has returned.

Going beyond the story
• Discuss the word 'nest'. List animals which make nests for themselves and their young. Talk about the various nests and what they are made from. Add illustrations.

• Compare the basic needs of humans and chimpanzees. Emphasise how young animals and/or children feel when they are alone.

• Make a mural or a book of places where animals and people rest and sleep.

Developing specific skills
• Reinforce directionality and return sweep.
• Focus on the concept of 'up'.
• Full stop — talk about the punctuation symbol, name and meaning.
• Pattern voice intonation to increase meaning.

Using the blackline master
• Read the text with the children.
• Demonstrate how to trace over and complete the word 'up'.
• Talk about the important details that the children should include in their illustration.

My name is _____

Look!

Here is Mother Chimp.

Look!

Here is Little Chimp

up   up   up   _____   _____

Little Chimp is _____ in the tree.

Mother Chimp is _____ in the tree.

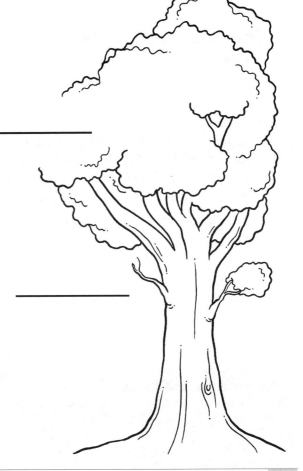

Here Comes Little Chimp

About the story
This is the second book in the series about Little Chimp. In this story, he is learning to climb a tree for the first time. Mother Chimp encourages Little Chimp and helps him to succeed.

Linking with other PM books
Climbing	PM Library Starters One
Tiger, Tiger	PM Library Red Level
The house in the tree	PM Library Blue Level

Creating the atmosphere
- Reread *Little Chimp* (Level 3) and talk about the characters, storyline and environment.
- Discuss with the children how they climb trees and their reasons for doing so. Talk about the similarities between Little Chimp and themselves.

Focusing on the story
- **Cover** Discuss why it is necessary for young chimpanzees to learn to climb trees.
- **Pages 2–7** Look closely at the various expressions on Little Chimp's face. How do the children think he is feeling? Predict what Little Chimp is going to say.
- **Pages 8–9** Read the text and compare it with the children's predictions.
- **Pages 10–11** Discuss how Little Chimp might react to Mother Chimp's encouragement. Talk about how Mother Chimp is similar to human mothers.

- **Pages 12–16** Discuss how Little Chimp is feeling now that he has mastered this skill. Ask, 'How do you think Mother Chimp is feeling?'

Going beyond the story
- Discuss the ways in which the children have overcome their fears when attempting a skill for the first time, and how their parents or a friend may have helped them.
- List the things that a five-year-old child can do independently. Have the children paint or draw a picture of themselves. Add statements.

Developing specific skills
- Reinforce directionality and return sweep.
- Encourage picture interpretation. Focus on the details that help to predict text.
- Revise one-to-one matching.

Using the blackline master
- Demonstrate how to trace over and complete the word 'little'.
- Read the text with the children.
- Discuss the details that are necessary to complete the illustration.

My name is _____

| Little | Little | Little | _____ |
| little | little | little | _____ |

Little Chimp said,

"I am too _____

to come up the tree."

Mother Chimp said,

"Come on,

_____ Chimp."

Jack and Billy

About the story
This is the second book in the series about Jack and Billy. Jack has made a car by painting a box and is very happy to share it with his brother. But Billy wants his own car and Jack helps him to achieve this.

Linking with other PM books
Playing	PM Library Starters One
The go-karts	PM Library Starters One
Bumper cars	PM Library Red Level

Creating the atmosphere
Reread *Photo Time* (Level 3). Discuss the characters of Jack and Billy and relate each boy's behaviour to his age.

Focusing on the story
- **Cover** Have the children identify Jack and Billy. Predict the storyline from the cover illustration.

- **Pages 2–7** Name the parts of the car that Jack has painted on his box and discuss imaginative play with the children.

- **Pages 8–9** Talk about the concept of sharing in relation to Jack's offer. Predict Billy's reaction based on his age and character (portrayed in *Photo Time*).

- **Pages 10–11** Read the text and compare it with the children's predictions.

- **Pages 12–16** Discuss Jack's solution to Billy's problem.

Going beyond the story
- Make small model cars (or other vehicles) from environmental materials.

- Use large boxes to make cars similar to those in the book. Have the children paint on their various features.

- Join large boxes together to make vans, trucks, trains, boats, etc. Paint or paste on wheels, lights, steering wheels, etc.

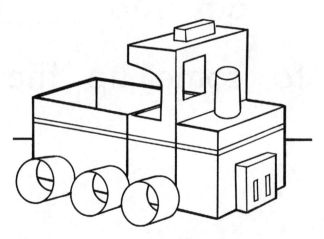

Developing specific skills
- Speech marks — talk about the punctuation symbol, name and meaning.
- Encourage picture interpretation. Focus on the details that help to predict text.
- Pattern voice intonation to increase meaning.

Using the blackline master
- Demonstrate how to trace over and complete the word 'in'.
- Read the sentences with the children and relate them to the pictures.
- Look carefully at the cars on page 16 of the text. Ask the children to colour the cars as they appear in the book. Have them draw in wheels, bumpers and lights.

My name is _____

in   in   in   _____   _____

Jack is in the car.

"Here I come _____ my car," said Jack.

Billy is in the car.

"Here I come _____ my car," said Billy.

Sam's Balloon

About the story
This is the second story about Sam who will become a familiar character in the PM Plus Story Books. In this story, Sam and her mother are at a fair when Sam sees a clown with some balloons.

Linking with other PM books
Balloons   PM Plus Level 1
Sam and Bingo   PM Plus Level 3
Birthday balloons   PM Library Blue Level

Creating the atmosphere
Provide each child with a balloon. Show them how to inflate it. Using a non-toxic marker pen, help the children to write their own name on their balloon. Display the balloons in the classroom.

Focusing on the story
- **Cover** Point out Sam and her mother. Identify them as the same characters featured in *Sam and Bingo*. Read the title together. Discuss the illustration. Count the balloons in the title-page illustration and identify each colour.

- **Pages 2–3** Examine the illustration. Ask, 'What do you think the clown and the child are talking about?' Point out that Mum has her back to the clown.

- **Pages 4–7** Notice Sam's agitation as the clown gives the balloons to the other children. Some children will be able to relate to the mathematical concept of subtraction. Model Sam's agitated voice as you read the text with the children.

- **Pages 8–9** Sam's disappointment is obvious from her body language and the text in bold. Discuss how she is feeling.

- **Pages 10–11** Talk about Sam's feelings when she sees the balloon that the clown has pulled from his pocket.

- **Pages 12–14** Point out Sam's interest and growing excitement.

- **Page 16** Discuss why Sam looks so happy. Remind the children about Sam's own dog, Bingo, from the earlier story *Sam and Bingo*.

Going beyond the story
- Ask the children to draw four balloons on light card. Have them colour the balloons the same as those in the book. The children can then cut out each balloon shape and staple coloured wool or string to it. Encourage them to use their shapes to demonstrate the subtraction process.

- Have the children paint colourful pictures of clowns holding bunches of balloons.

Developing specific skills
- Encourage picture interpretation.
- Pattern voice intonation to assist meaning.
- Speech marks — talk about the punctuation symbol, name and meaning.

Using the blackline master
- Talk about the letters in the word 'look'.
- Link the pictures with the sentences.
- Encourage the children to study the illustration of the balloon twisted into the shape of a dog (see page 16 of the text) before they draw their own picture.

My name is _____

Look   Look   Look   _____

Look at
the clown.

Look at
the balloons.

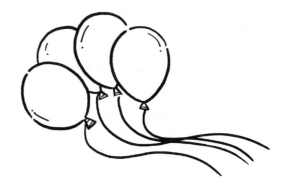

Look!

My balloon
is a dog.

Baby Wakes Up

About the story
A new character is introduced in this book and the story is told in the 'first person'. Here the girl amuses the baby when they both wake up earlier than their parents.

Linking with other PM books
Our baby	PM Library Non-fiction Yellow Level
My little sister	PM Library Non-fiction Yellow/Blue Levels
Birthday balloons	PM Library Blue Level

Creating the atmosphere
Read *Our baby* and *My little sister* (PM Library Non-fiction Yellow Level). Discuss with the children how they interact with their younger brothers and/or sisters.

Focusing on the story
- **Cover** Discuss the dependence of babies on other family members and why they sleep in cots.
- **Pages 2–5** Talk about how these pages set the scene within the house. The girl can see that the baby and her parents are asleep.
- **Pages 6–9** Ask, 'What do you think the girl is going to do?'
- **Pages 10–13** Discuss the reasons why the girl has given the baby two teddy bears.
- **Pages 14–16** Ask, 'Why is the baby happy?' Talk about how helpful the girl has been.

Going beyond the story
- List toys that are appropriate for babies.
- Have the children paint or draw toys. Add captions, e.g. 'Here is a teddy bear for the baby.'
- Make a mural or class book of photos of the children when they were babies. Add appropriate captions.

Sally is asleep.
Sally is in a cot.

Here is Abdul
and his nana.

Developing specific skills
- Link the visual pattern and sound of the upper- and lower-case letters: Bb, Mm, Dd.
- Reinforce the pattern of the words: Baby, Mum, Dad.
- Understand the difference between a letter and a word.

Using the blackline master
- Demonstrate how to trace over the word 'is'.
- Read the text with the children.
- Have the children draw a matching picture for the last sentence.

My name is  _____

is   is   is   _____   _____

I am up.   Baby is asleep.

Mum is asleep.   Dad is asleep.

| is | is |  |

"Look, Baby.

Here _____

a little teddy bear."

"Look, Baby.

Here _____

a big teddy bear."

Blackline master 8 • *Baby Wakes Up* © Nelson, 2000.   *PM Plus Teachers' Guide: Levels 3–5*   49

This page may be photocopied for educational use within the purchasing institution.

STORY BOOKS LEVEL **3**

Running words: 55

The Big Hill

About the story

It is certain that birds evolved well before the end of the Cretaceous period. Cattle egrets that take ticks from modern hippos probably had ancestors that clambered on dinosaurs! This book is part realistic, part fiction.

Linking with other PM books

Big and little	PM Plus Level 2
Big things	PM Library Starters One
Little things	PM Library Starters One

Creating the atmosphere

Talk about the mathematical concepts of 'big' and 'little'. Record some of the things that seem very big to the children, e.g. '"My dad's truck is big," said Nick.'

Focusing on the story

- **Cover** Many children will recognise the words 'The' and 'Big' in the title. Remind them to use the initial letter and the illustration when attempting to decode the word 'Hill'.

- **Pages 2–5** Talk about the movements of the bird and the sun as it rises.

- **Pages 6–7** Look at the sun and how it is shining on the hill. Ask, 'Why is the bird resting on the hill?'

- **Pages 8–9** Link the text with the movement lines of the big hill. Discuss what is happening to Little Bird.

- **Pages 10–13** Read the text with the children in an expressive voice. Explain that the sun is higher in the sky now and is much hotter. The dinosaur has woken up because of the warmth from the sun.

- **Pages 14–16** Talk about the fact that Little Bird is in danger — it must escape. Encourage the children to use the illustrations to decode the word 'fly'.

Going beyond the story

- Make a large mural of animals waking up with the heat of the early morning sun. Have the children draw the animals, cut them out and paste them onto the mural. Add captions.

> The sun is up in the sky.
> The pig wakes up.
> The dog wakes up.
> The cat wakes up.
> The sun is hot.

- Read, sing and dance to *The bear went over the mountain* (PM Library Readalongs).

Developing specific skills

- Pattern voice intonation to increase meaning.
- Full stop — talk about the punctuation symbol, name and meaning.
- Reinforce the use of the initial letter to decode unknown words.

Using the blackline master

- Read each sentence with the children. Encourage them to say the word 'on' as they read.
- Link the visual pattern of the word 'on' with its sound.

My name is _____

on   on   on   _____   _____

Little Bird is up
_____ a dinosaur.

I am up
_____ a swing.

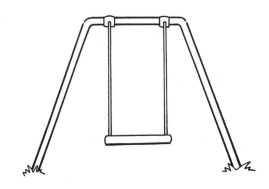

I am up
_____ a ladder.

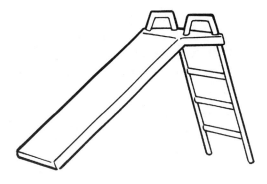

I am up
_____ a wall.

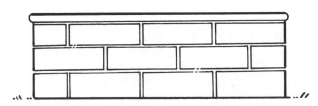

Teddy Bears' Picnic

About the story
Fantasy stories about toys appeal to a young child's imaginative world. In this story, Panda misses the bus to the Teddy Bears' Picnic.

Linking with other PM books
I am running	PM Plus Level 1
Up in the sky	PM Plus Level 1
Going out	PM Plus Level 2

Creating the atmosphere
Talk about picnics. Encourage the children to discuss these experiences. List some of the food and drink that were taken and the activities that were enjoyed.

Focusing on the story
- **Cover** Read the title using the initial letter 'P' and the illustration to decode the word 'Picnic'. Look closely at the details and predict the story content. Read the title on the title page.
- **Pages 2–3** Talk about the three bears. Have the children predict what their names might be. Confirm their predictions later in the text. Draw the children's attention to the wording and picture on the poster. Read the poster before reading the text.
- **Pages 4–7** Talk about the actions of Big Teddy and Little Teddy. Read the bus stop sign and the words on the bus. Develop the children's ability to take advantage of visual language.

- **Pages 8–11** Encourage the children to read the text using the appropriate intonation to reflect Panda's problem. Predict what Panda might have to do now.
- **Pages 12–16** Talk about the hot-air balloon as a method of transport. Enjoy the satisfying ending to Panda's dilemma.

Going beyond the story
- Read, sing and dance to *The bus song* (PM Library Readalongs).
- Give each child a balloon to inflate. Using coloured non-toxic marker pens, have them decorate and write their name on the balloon. Attach the balloons to empty yogurt containers and suspend these 'hot-air' balloons attractively. Some children may like to write a caption alongside their displayed balloon.

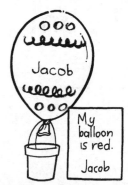

Developing specific skills
- Associate the upper- and lower-case initial letters in: Bear, bus, balloon; Panda, picnic.
- Exclamation mark — introduce the punctuation symbol, name and meaning.
- Reinforce directionality and return sweep.

Using the blackline master
- Read the sentences with the children allowing them to say the words 'on' or 'in' as appropriate.
- Encourage verbalisation of the words 'on' and 'in' as they are copied onto the blackline master.
- Have the children draw Big Teddy, Little Teddy and Panda in the appropriate illustrations.

My name is _____

on   on

Big Teddy is _____ the bus.

Little Teddy is _____ the bus.

in

Panda is up
_____ the balloon.

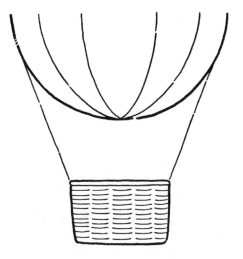

My Tower

About the story
Most children will have had experiences of building with blocks. The little girl's disappointment turns into triumph as she becomes aware of the logical process of stacking blocks of different sizes.

Linking with other PM books
Up in the sky	PM Plus Level 2
Up and down	PM Plus Level 2
Tall things	PM Library Non-fiction Red/Yellow Levels

Creating the atmosphere
Ask the children to count out ten building blocks of different sizes and to stack them as a tower. Discuss any problems that may have occurred.

Focusing on the story
- **Cover** Talk about the girl and her actions. Ask the children what she might be building.
- **Pages 2–3** Encourage the children to notice the unstable stack of blocks and to predict what might happen.
- **Pages 4–5** Model how to read the text with the appropriate intonation. Discuss what the girl should do to make her construction stable.
- **Pages 6–13** Study each illustration commenting on the girl's more logical stacking method before reading the text.
- **Pages 14–15** Talk about the last block to go on the tower. Point out the concentration and anxiety on the girl's face. Predict whether this last block will upset the stability of the tower.
- **Page 16** Enjoy the girl's sense of achievement and read the text in a way that reflects her pleasure.

Going beyond the story
- Encourage the children to make models using coloured plastic blocks. Share these models in small group situations. Have each child to give a detailed explanation.
- Invite the children to draw pictures of things that go up, e.g. a plane, a bird, etc. Help them to write a suitable caption. Include the words 'is going up'.

Developing specific skills
- Understand the difference between a letter and a word.
- Exclamation mark — talk about the punctuation symbol, name and meaning.
- Encourage picture interpretation. Focus on the details that help to predict the text.

Using the blackline master
- Read the sentence encouraging the children to say the word 'up'.
- Using a finger, 'write' the word 'up' in the air with large flowing movements.
- Ask the children to colour the blocks the same colour as in the book.

My name is _____

| up | up | up |

My tower is going

_____ and _____ and _____.

Look at my big tower.

Running words: 63

My Book

About the story
In this story, the third in the series, the girl is looking for a book that she has been reading. While she is looking, she finds three of her toys. Finally, she discovers her book and reads it to the toys.

Linking with other PM books

Tiger, Tiger	PM Library Red Level
Ben's teddy bear	PM Library Red Level
Where are the sunhats?	PM Library Yellow Level

Creating the atmosphere

- Reread *Baby Wakes Up* and *My Tower* (Levels 3 and 4). Talk about the character who features in these books.

- Encourage the children to talk about their favourite books and the books they like to read by themselves. Have them name the places where they like to read, the places where they keep their books and the people that they read to.

Focusing on the story

- **Cover** Predict the storyline from the cover illustration. Discuss the vignette on the title page and the fact that this is the book the little girl is reading on the cover.

- **Pages 2–3** Examine the illustration and discuss the places where a book might be. Look specifically for the lost book.

- **Pages 4–13** Talk about the fact that we often find something else when we are looking for a particular object, and how we are then distracted from our main

task. Help the children to use the picture clues to decode the words 'elephant', 'monkey' and 'tiger'.

- **Pages 14–16** Discuss the girl's satisfaction as she locates her favourite book and reads to her toys.

Going beyond the story

- Encourage the children to talk about losing and finding their own books and toys. List places where they were found.

- Ask the children to write the name of a book they like to read on card. Have them then copy the last line from *My Book* and add the names of people they like to read to.

Developing specific skills

- Encourage reasoning and prediction. Ask, 'What do you think …?'
- Talk about first and last letters of a word.
- Notice the letters and hear the sounds at the end of the words: look, book.

Using the blackline master

- Read the text with the children.
- Demonstrate how to trace over and complete the word 'my'.
- Have the children draw themselves looking for their lost book. They can then colour the toys and the book as they appear in the story.

My name is _____

my   my   my   _____   _____

I am looking for my book.

Here is my elephant.

Here is _____ monkey.

Here is _____ tiger.

Here is _____ book.

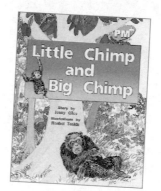

Little Chimp and Big Chimp

About the story
This is the third story in the PM Plus series about Little Chimp. In this story, he is slightly older and becoming more adventurous. He is mastering the skills of climbing trees and swinging from branch to branch.

Linking with other PM books
Little Chimp	PM Plus Level 3
Here Comes Little Chimp	PM Plus Level 3
Tiger, Tiger	PM Library Red Level

Creating the atmosphere
• Reread *Little Chimp* and *Here Comes Little Chimp* (Level 3).

• Using *Monkeys and Apes* (PM Library Animal Facts Turquoise Level) read the section on chimpanzees and discuss the skills that Little Chimp may be mastering.

Focusing on the story
• **Cover** Talk about Big Chimp and what he is doing. Read the title with the children.

• **Pages 2–5** Discuss the fact that Little Chimp can now swing from tree to tree.

• **Pages 6–7** Focus on the new character, Big Chimp, and what he is doing.

• **Pages 8–11** Look at the large branch that Little Chimp is swinging up to and predict what may happen.

• **Pages 12–13** Discuss the accuracy of the children's predictions.

• **Pages 14–16** Talk about the other options Little Chimp could have taken after he woke Big Chimp.

Going beyond the story
• Discuss with the children the physical skills that they have mastered at various stages in their lives, e.g. jumping, skipping, swinging, climbing, riding, etc. Point out that practice is an important part of mastering a skill.

• Have the children draw themselves doing a skill that they have finally mastered. Add captions.

Developing specific skills
• Pattern voice intonation to increase meaning.
• Encourage picture interpretation. Focus on the details that help to predict text.
• Exclamation mark — talk about the punctuation symbol, name and meaning.

Using the blackline master
• Demonstrate how to trace over and complete the word 'Big'. Point out the upper-case letter and why it has been used.
• Read the sentences with the children. Talk about the important details that should be added to each illustration.

My name is _____

Big   Big   Big   _____

Here is Big chimp.

Big Chimp is asleep
in the sun.

Down comes Little Chimp.

_____ Chimp wakes up.

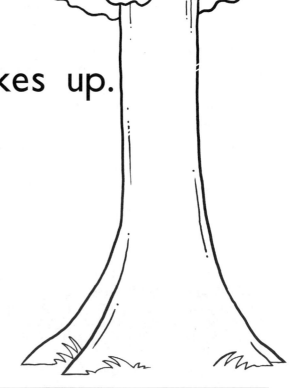

_____ Chimp
is looking
for Little Chimp.

Sam's Race

About the story

This is the third story in the PM Plus series about Sam. In this story, Sam is taking part in a running race. All is well until she trips over. One-to-one matching is an additional feature of this book.

Linking with other PM books

I am running   PM Plus Level 1
Sam and Bingo   PM Plus Level 3
Sam's Balloon   PM Plus Level 3

Creating the atmosphere

Take the children outside to a grassed area for a running race. Alternatively, have a discussion about running in a race. Talk about the starting line, the finishing line, getting ready, listening for the starter's signal, etc.

Focusing on the story

- **Cover** Identify Sam and read her name in the title. Use the illustration and the initial letter 'R' to decode the word 'Race'. Read the title again on the title page and talk about the vignette of Sam.

- **Pages 2–5** Point out Sam and her mother — both recognisable by their hair colour and their actions. Talk about the one-to-one matching of a child to an adult.

- **Pages 6–9** Demonstrate how to read the text with intonation.

- **Pages 10–11** Encourage the children to predict what might happen next.

- **Pages 12–16** Talk about Sam's positive attitude to her predicament and how she succeeded in the end.

Going beyond the story

- Read the story *The Hare and the Tortoise* (PM Library Traditional Tales and Plays Purple Level) to the children. Talk about the tortoise's determination in this race.

- Have the children draw a picture of themselves succeeding at some skill they have been trying very hard to master. Display these pictures as a wall story. Help the children to write their own captions.

Developing specific skills

- Recognise the following initial letters within the context of the story: r — race, ran; Gg — Good, girl.
- Use *sh* (PM Library Alphabet Blends) to develop the sound: sh — shouted.
- Talk about first and last letters of a word.

Using the blackline master

- Read the sentences with the children.
- Demonstrate how to trace over the word 'come'.
- Talk about the important details that the children should include in their illustrations.

My name is _____

come   come   come   _____

"Mum! Mum!

Here I come," shouted Sam.

"Come on, Sam!" shouted Mum.

"Come on!"

Jack's Birthday

About the story
This is the third story in the PM Plus series about Jack and Billy. In this story, Jack receives a new car for his birthday from his mother and father. Billy is envious and the car disappears. Dad comes to the rescue and all is well.

Linking with other PM books
Birthday balloons   PM Library Blue Level
Baby Bear's present   PM Library Blue Level
Down by the station   PM Library Readalongs

Creating the atmosphere
Reread *Photo Time* and *Jack and Billy* (Level 3). Discuss the characters of Jack and Billy. Talk about how children feel when they are opening presents.

Focusing on the story
- **Cover** Children will recognise Jack and Billy from previous books. Talk about the game Jack is playing with his car.
- **Pages 2–7** Discuss the present that Jack has received for his birthday and how young children react to siblings receiving presents. Comment on the fact that Billy is watching Jack.
- **Pages 8–9** Observe this illustration closely. Discuss what both boys are doing.
- **Pages 10–11** Have the children predict what has happened to the car based on the previous illustration and their experiences with younger siblings.
- **Pages 12–16** Discuss how Dad is involved in solving Jack's problem.

Going beyond the story
- Invite the children to talk about their birthdays and presents that they have received. Have them draw or paint their presents and write captions.
- In the classroom, have the children make a garage with blocks. Extend them further by asking them to make a road for the toy vehicles to travel along. Captions can be used to describe the cars in the garage.

The little cars go up here.

Here is the little bus.

Here is the blue truck.

Developing specific skills
- Link the visual pattern and sound of the initial upper-case letters: M — Mum, D — Dad, J — Jack, B — Billy.
- Encourage picture interpretation. Focus on the details that help to predict text.
- Pattern voice intonation to increase meaning.

Using the blackline master
- Demonstrate how to trace over and complete the word 'said'.
- Read the sentences with the children.
- Talk about the details needed when the children draw their own illustration.

My name is _____

said   said   said   _____

"A car for me," said Jack.

"My car can go up and down," _____ Jack.

"Here is a garage for my red car," _____ Jack.

Bedtime

About the story

Jack and Billy are becoming familiar characters. In this story, Jack tries delaying tactics when it is time for bed. However, the pleasure of a bedtime story with Mum has him changing his mind very quickly.

Linking with other PM books

Photo Time	PM Plus Level 3
Jack and Billy	PM Plus Level 3
Jack's Birthday	PM Plus Level 4

Creating the atmosphere

Talk about getting ready for bed — the family routines and the quiet activities. Some children may like to talk about a baby in the family or their older brothers and sisters, and how their bedtime routine differs from their own.

Focusing on the story

- **Cover** Identify the characters Jack, Billy and Mum from the previous stories in the PM Plus series.

- **Pages 2–5** Discuss Mum's comment and Jack's reply.

- **Pages 6–7** Ask the children why Jack isn't taking any notice of Mum and is continuing to play with his car.

- **Pages 8–11** Talk about Billy's comments. Predict what Jack might do now.

- **Pages 12–13** Ask, 'Why is Jack standing at the door?'

- **Pages 14–16** Ask, 'Why did Jack decide to go to bed after all?'

Going beyond the story

- List the children's favourite bedtime stories. Have them draw a picture from their favourite story. Display these pictures with suitable captions.

- Make a simple three-part booklet which summarises the story. The following captions could be used:

  1 'Come to bed, Jack,' said Mum.

  2 'Here is my book,' said Billy.

  3 Jack and Billy and Mum are looking at the book.

Have the children complete the booklet by adding illustrations.

Developing specific skills

- Associate upper- and lower-case letters: Bb.
- Talk about first and last letters of a word.
- Encourage picture interpretation. Focus on the details that help to predict text.

Using the blackline master

- Read the words in the boxes with the children. Point out the same initial letter for each word.
- Encourage the children to read their sentences aloud as they fill in the missing words.
- Have them draw a picture of themselves in the bed reading a book.

My name is _____

| book | Billy | bed |

"Look at me, Mum,"
said _____.

"I am in _____."

"Mum! Mum!
Come here," said Billy.
Here is my _____."

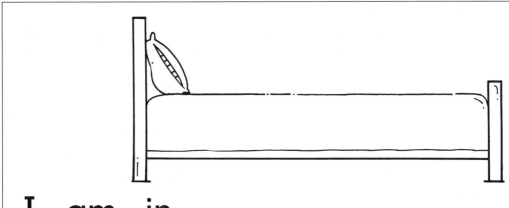

I am in _____.
Look at my _____.

The Lucky Dip

About the story
Two new characters, Matthew and Emma, who are twins, are introduced in this story. The fun and often the disappointment of a gift from a lucky dip is portrayed in this book.

Linking with other PM books
Jack's Birthday — PM Plus Level 4
Ben's treasure hunt — PM Library Red Level
Look up, look down — PM Library Non-fiction Red/Yellow Levels

Creating the atmosphere
Wrap some small items of classroom equipment, e.g. plastic blocks, crayons, etc. in newspaper and place them in a box containing shredded paper. Invite the children to choose an item, then guess what might be inside.

Focusing on the story
- **Cover** Talk about the children's excitement as they reach into the lucky dip. Introduce the characters Matthew and Emma. Write their names clearly on a chart. Read the title on the cover and on the title page.
- **Pages 2–3** Model how to read the text in a way that reflects the excitement of the illustration. Draw the children's attention to the exclamation marks.
- **Pages 4–7** Ask the children why Matthew and Emma look so disappointed when they unwrap a comb and a toothbrush.
- **Pages 8–9** Point out Matthew's thoughtful expression.

- **Pages 10–11** Ask, 'Why do Mum and Dad look happy about their gifts?' Point out Emma placing the paper in the bin.
- **Pages 12–16** Talk about Dad's teasing expression and the children's satisfaction in the end.

Going beyond the story
- Look at the expressions on Matthew and Emma's faces on pages 4–9. Compare these with their expressions on pages 12–16. Choose either character, and on a piece of folded paper draw and write about the unhappy and the happy expressions. This activity will help children understand cause and effect.

- Role-play the story, improvising with additional dialogue.

Developing specific skills
- Discuss these upper-case letters: M, D, E, H, L, T, A.
- Speech marks — talk about the punctuation symbol, name and meaning.
- Encourage reasoning and prediction. Ask, 'What do you think …?'

Using the blackline master
- Use the books c, t and b (PM Library Alphabet Starters) to reinforce each letter's sound and shape.
- Trace over the letters: c, t, b.
- Say the name of each picture and write its initial letter or attempt the whole word.

My name is _____

| c | t | b |

Here is a comb.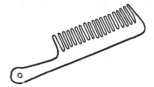

Look at the toothbrush.

Here is a little blue car.

Look at my teddy bear.

c   c   c   c   c

t   t   t   t   t

b   b   b   b   b

Running words: 82

Let's Pretend

About the story

This is the second story about the twins, Matthew and Emma. Mum is painting the children's faces as she prepares them for a fancy dress party. Matthew's initial disappointment eventually turns to delight.

Linking with other PM books

The Lucky Dip	PM Plus Level 4
The play	PM Plus Level 1
Dressing-up	PM Library Starters One

Creating the atmosphere

Show the children a book with examples of face painting. Encourage them to talk about their favourite design and to explain why they chose it.

Focusing on the story

- **Cover** Talk about the costumes that Matthew and Emma are wearing and about their face paint. Read the title to the children. Comment on the initial letters 'L' and 'P'. Read the title again on the title page and discuss the vignette of face paints.

- **Pages 2–3** Compare the apprehension on Matthew's face with Emma's obvious joy.

- **Pages 4–5** Ask, 'Why do you think Matthew is unhappy?'

- **Pages 6–7** Encourage the children to read the text with the appropriate intonation.

- **Pages 8–9** Ask, 'Why do you think Matthew is showing Mum the picture of the tiger?'

- **Pages 10–11** Ensure that the children understand what Mum is doing to Matthew now.

- **Pages 12–16** Talk about both Matthew's and Emma's feelings.

Going beyond the story

- Cut out cardboard shapes the same size as the children's faces. Have each child paint their cardboard shape. Display these 'painted faces' with written explanations.

"I am a big fierce lion," said Ling.

- Hold a special 'Dress-up Day'. Invite parents to join in the fun and to help with painting the children's faces.

- Study some coloured photographs of wild animals. Talk about their features and the markings that make them distinct from other animals.

Developing specific skills

- Encourage reasoning and prediction. Ask, 'Why do you think ...?'
- Link picture and initial letter.
- Pattern voice intonation to increase meaning.

Using the blackline master

- Use the books *r*, *b* and *t* (PM Library Alphabet Starters) to reinforce each sound.
- Say the name of each picture on the blackline master. Write the initial letter in the box.
- Read each sentence and fill in the correct word.

My name is _____

| r | b | t |

| bear | tiger |

"I am a big _____,"
said Emma.

"I am a _____,"
said Matthew.

Red Puppy

About the story

Many children will be able to relate to the theme of this story — the feeling of anguish when you are the last person to be chosen. Red Puppy seemed to be the odd one out in a basket of toys.

Linking with other PM books

The toy box	PM Plus Level 1
A home for Little Teddy	PM Library Red Level
Tim's favourite toy	PM Library Blue Level

Creating the atmosphere

Bring a pocket-sized soft toy to school. Encourage the children to handle it while the story is being read and discussed.

Focusing on the story

- **Cover** Discuss the cover illustration and read the title. Draw the children's attention to the capital 'R' and 'P' at the beginning of each word. Read the title again on the title page and talk about the vignette of Red Puppy.

- **Pages 2–5** Encourage the children to use the vignettes when decoding words. Emphasise the importance of picture and initial letter link.

- **Pages 6–11** Point out the one-to-one matching of each child carrying a toy. Ask the children to read the bold type with extra emphasis.

- **Pages 12–13** Emotional involvement in a text helps children to make meaning of their world. Ask, 'How would you feel if you were never chosen?'

- **Pages 14–15** Ask the children to read the text and predict what might happen.

- **Page 16** Link the text and the illustration.

Going beyond the story

- Hold a 'Small Toy Day' at school. Ask the children to bring along their favourite small toy. Encourage them to describe their toy to a friend or to a small group. Display the toys in a large basket. Each toy could have a label with its name and a brief description.

- Have the children paint pictures of Red Puppy. Help them to write a sentence about him.

Developing specific skills

- Understand that bold type should be read with emphasis.
- Notice the letters and hear the sounds at the end of the words: Puppy, teddy, happy.
- Encourage picture interpretation. Focus on the details that help to predict the text.

Using the blackline master

- Talk about the letters in the word 'are'.
- Read each sentence saying the missing word — 'are'.
- Draw each set of toys in their appropriate position in the basket.

My name is _____

are   are   are

The teddy bears
_____ in the basket.

The rabbits
_____ in the basket.

The dolls
_____ in the basket.

Red Puppy
is in the basket, too.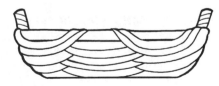

Mother Bird

About the story

The illustrations and the text which is written in the present tense, show the actions of both the bird and the cat.

Linking with other PM books

Pussy and the birds   PM Library Red Level
My little cat   PM Plus Level 2
Making a bird   PM Plus Non-fiction Level 1

Creating the atmosphere

Read a story or poem to the children in which a cat preys upon a bird. Talk about the behaviour of both the cat and the bird.

Focusing on the story

- **Cover** Read the title and discuss the cover illustration. Talk about Mother Bird's actions both on the cover and the title page.

- **Pages 2–7** Read the text and discuss the need for Mother Bird to find food for her babies.

- **Pages 8–9** Have the children predict what Mother Bird will do.

- **Pages 10–11** Encourage the children to read the text with urgent voices to reflect the meaning.

- **Pages 12–16** Discuss how Mother Bird has been able to outwit the cat and reach the baby birds just in time.

Going beyond the story

- Reread *Making a bird* (PM Plus Non-fiction Level 1). Have the children follow the instructions and make a bird.

- Listen to recorded music of bird calls.

- Read, dance and sing along to *Over in the meadow* (PM Library Readalongs). Draw and cut out pictures of the mother animals with their babies. Paste these on to a mural made of collage materials.

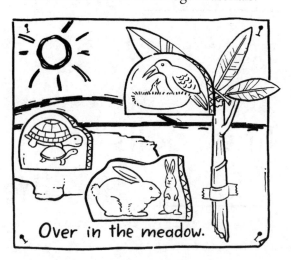

Over in the meadow.

Developing specific skills

- Notice the letters and hear the sounds at the end of the words: looks, comes, sees, goes.
- Full stop — talk about the punctuation symbol at the end of both long and short sentences.
- Revise upper- and lower-case letters: Mm, Bb, Hh, Tt.

Using the blackline master

- Point to and say each upper- and lower-case letter. Show the children how to link the letters with a coloured pencil.
- Write the lower-case letter alongside its matching upper-case letter.
- Read the sentences and trace over the initial letters. Draw the last picture.

My name is _____

H	m	t	T

| | B | h | M | b |

B____   H____   M____   T____

Mother Bird is looking for a worm.

The baby birds are hungry.

Here comes a cat.

Kitty Cat and the Fish

About the story
Kitty Cat's mischievous nature leads her into trouble with her owner and with Fat Cat, once again.

Linking with other PM books
My little cat	PM Plus Level 2
Fishing	PM Library Starters Two
Father Bear goes fishing	PM Library Red Level

Creating the atmosphere
Reintroduce the characters Kitty Cat and Fat Cat by rereading *Kitty Cat* (Level 3).

Focusing on the story
- **Cover** Talk about the illustration. Read the title with the children. Observe their use of the picture clue and the initial letter to decode the word 'fish'. Encourage the children to share their own experiences of cat and kitten behaviour.
- **Pages 2–7** Predict what Kitty Cat might do next before turning each page.
- **Pages 8–9** Ask, 'Who does the hand belong to?' Model how this page should be read. Discuss the purpose of the exclamation marks.
- **Pages 10–11** Ask, 'Who do the legs and feet belong to?' Observe the children as they read the word 'safe'.
- **Pages 12–13** Talk about Fat Cat's actions. Predict what Kitty Cat might do next.

- **Pages 14–15** Ask the children how they think Fat Cat will react.
- **Page 16** Ask, 'How is Fat Cat feeling? Is Kitty Cat scared? Why/Why not?'

Going beyond the story
- Ask the children to draw and write about the two parts to the story — Kitty Cat and the little fish, and Fat Cat and the big fish.

- Encourage the children to share personal experiences about going fishing. They could read and talk about the family who goes fishing in *Fishing* (PM Library Starters Two).

Developing specific skills
- Exclamation mark — talk about the punctuation symbol, name and meaning.
- Encourage reasoning and prediction. Ask, 'Why do you think …? How will …?'
- Notice the letters and hear the sounds at the end of the word: look*ing*.

Using the blackline master
- Talk about the opposites 'big' and 'little'. Read each sentence and have the children write the correct word.
- Have the children draw the fish in the bowl and in the pond.

My name is _____

| big | little |

Kitty Cat is looking at the _____ fish.

Fat Cat is looking at the _____ fish.

A dog  is _____.

A puppy is _____.

A cat  is _____.

A kitten is _____.

Bingo's Ice Cream

About the story

This is another story about Sam and her dog, Bingo. The setting is a small shopping centre. Mum comes out of the shop with ice creams when the inevitable happens!

Linking with other PM books

Sam and Bingo series	PM Plus Levels 3 and 4
Four ice-creams	PM Library Starters Two
sh	PM Library Alphabet Blends

Creating the atmosphere

Reread *Sam and Bingo*, *Sam's Balloon* and *Sam's Race* (Levels 3 and 4). Ask the children to paint a picture of Sam and a picture of Bingo. Display each painting with a descriptive sentence, e.g. 'Sam has curly red hair', 'Bingo is a little dog.'

Focusing on the story

• **Cover** Discuss the illustration. Talk about the ice cream that Mum is giving to Sam. Point out the sign and the pictures on the shop window. Read the title together. Read it again on the title page.

• **Page 2** Discuss why Sam is standing with her arms outstretched.

• **Page 4** Notice how Bingo is looking up at the ice creams.

• **Pages 6–9** Predict what Sam could be saying. Ask, 'What do you think Mum will do now?'

• **Pages 10–13** Talk about how Sam is feeling. Discuss Bingo's actions.

• **Pages 14–16** Discuss the satisfying ending to the story. Comment on the one-to-one matching of the text and illustration on page 16.

Going beyond the story

• Make a list of the children's favourite ice creams. Have them draw, cut out and paste their ice cream onto a chart under the appropriate heading.

• Role-play the story, improvising with additional dialogue.

• Draw pictures of family members holding an ice cream each. Reinforce the one-to-one matching.

Developing specific skills

• Understand the concept of first and last words.
• Associate upper- and lower-case letters: Hh — Here, here; Aa — And, and.
• Use *sh* (PM Library Alphabet Blends) to develop the sound: sh — shouted.

Using the blackline master

• Read each sentence together. Have the children write in the missing words.
• Reinforce the importance of drawing an illustration to match the text.

My name is _____

for	for	for

Sam said,
"An ice cream _____ me,
and an ice cream _____ you,
and an ice cream
_____ Bingo, too."

I said,
"This ice cream
is _____ me."

Baby Panda

About the story
This story about dangers that face baby pandas in the wild is full of true facts and is of high interest.

Linking with other PM books
Teddy Bears' Picnic	PM Plus Level 3
Mother Bird	PM Plus Level 4
Run, Rabbit, Run!	PM Plus Level 5

Creating the atmosphere
Show the children photographs of pandas in the wild or read them the story *Pandas in the Mountains* (PM Library Gold Level). Talk about the panda's thick coat and its black markings.

Focusing on the story
- **Cover** Read the title. Talk about Mother Panda holding Baby Panda and the way they are interacting.
- **Pages 2–5** Discuss why Mother Panda doesn't know that Baby Panda has rolled down the slope.
- **Pages 6–9** Ask, 'Why can't Mother Panda see Baby Panda?'
- **Pages 10–11** Assist the children to understand that this is a wild mountain cat and not a large domestic cat. Talk about the terrible danger that Baby Panda is now in.
- **Pages 12–15** Discuss the reason why the big cat runs away when it sees Mother Panda.

- **Page 16** Give children time to savour the emotions on the last page.

Going beyond the story
- Record the text from the story onto six sheets of A4 paper. Provide each child or group with one page of text to illustrate. Encourage them to read the book again to find their particular section of the story. When the sheets have been illustrated, paste them in order onto the six sides of a cardboard box. The children will enjoy reading their 'Panda Box'.

- Make a class book featuring photographs from magazines about animal mothers and their babies.

Developing specific skills
- Ensure correct directionality on double-page spreads.
- Question mark — introduce the punctuation symbol, name and meaning.
- Talk about first and last letters of a word.

Using the blackline master
- Read the words 'runs', 'looks' and 'sees' aloud. Talk about the common sound at the end of each word.
- Read the sentences aloud. Have the children write in the correct words.
- Discuss ideas for the picture. Reinforce the importance of the text matching the illustration.

My name is _____

runs   looks   sees

Mother Panda _____ for Baby Panda.

The big cat _____ Baby Panda.

Mother Panda _____ down the hill.

Here comes Baby Panda.

Monkey on the Roof

About the story
The twins, Matthew and Emma, are playing outside with a toy when they throw it too high and it lands on the roof of the house. They are faced with the problem of how to retrieve their toy.

Linking with other PM books

The Lucky Dip	PM Plus Level 4
Let's Pretend	PM Plus Level 4
My little sister	PM Library Non-fiction Yellow/Blue Levels

Creating the atmosphere

Talk about throwing and catching games that children often play with balls. Discuss what happens if a ball is thrown too high or out of reach.

Focusing on the story

- **Cover** Discuss the cover illustration. Many children will recognise the twins from the two previous stories *The Lucky Dip* and *Let's Pretend* (Level 4). Read the title with the children. Point out the toy monkey.

- **Pages 2–5** Talk about Matthew's and Emma's actions. Allow the children time to describe similar situations that they have experienced.

- **Pages 6–7** Have the children predict what might happen next.

- **Pages 8–9** Ask, 'What do you think Mum will say to Matthew?'

- **Pages 10–11** Ask, 'Why didn't Mum let Matthew go up on the roof?'

- **Pages 12–13** Point out the safety precautions that Mum has taken with the ladder.

- **Pages 14–16** Enjoy Emma's mischievous remarks.

Going beyond the story

- Make a list of the games that the children like to play at home with their brothers and/or sisters. Use a repetitive style of sentence that includes the word 'said' and speech marks.

> "I play tag with my sister," said Anna.
> "I play hide-and-seek,"

- Discuss various situations around the home that may be potentially dangerous for young children.

Developing specific skills
- Comma — introduce the punctuation symbol, name and meaning.
- Speech marks and exclamation mark — talk about the punctuation symbol for each.
- Reinforce directionality and return sweep of longer sentences.

Using the blackline master
- Point out the capital 'M' for each word in the boxes.
- Read each sentence with the children encouraging them to focus on the meaning of the text.
- Have the children draw a picture to match the last two sentences.

My name is _____

| Matthew | Monkey | Mum |

"Oh!" said Emma.
"Look at _____."

"I can see Monkey,"
said _____.

Mum went up
the ladder.
"Here he is!"
said _____.

Run, Rabbit, Run!

About the story
This book is about a hungry dog and a vulnerable little rabbit. It has the strong thread of reality that evokes fear and tension.

Linking with other PM books
Mother Bird	PM Plus Level 4
Baby Panda	PM Plus Level 5
Lizard loses his tail	PM Library Red Level

Creating the atmosphere
Using the photograph of a real rabbit on page 29 of *A first alphabet book* (PM Library), discuss its features. Talk about its long ears, whiskers, fur, etc. Draw the children's attention to its burrow.

Focusing on the story
- **Cover** Discuss the running action of the rabbit. Read the title with meaning. Talk about the initial capital letter 'R'.
- **Pages 2–3** Ensure that the children understand the meaning of 'Rabbit Hill'. Identify Little Rabbit.
- **Pages 4–7** Point out that rabbits usually like eating short grass best.
- **Pages 8–13** The tension of the story increases as the large dog chases Little Rabbit. Observe the children as they attempt to decode the word 'running'.
- **Pages 14–16** Talk about the safety of Little Rabbit's burrow.

Going beyond the story
- Assist the children to identify the three main parts of the story. Record them on a chart, for example:

  1 Little Rabbit is eating grass.

  2 Here comes a big dog.

  3 Little Rabbit is running home.

  Have the children copy these sentences and draw matching pictures. Emphasise the importance of the illustration matching the text.

- Make a mural of Rabbit Hill. The rabbits could be made from light card and decorated with material and wool. Record sentences from the story on the mural for extra reading practice.

Developing specific skills
- Understand the concept of first and last words.
- Question mark — introduce the punctuation symbol, name and meaning.
- Scan words for endings, e.g. rabbit*s*, look*ing*, eat*ing*, come*s*, goe*s*.

Using the blackline master
- Encourage the children to say the words 'look' and 'looking'. Have them listen to the additional sound and point out the extra letters.
- Read the sentences aloud. Ensure that the children understand that the text should make sense.
- Have the children draw Little Rabbit running home.

My name is _____

look	looking

Look at the rabbits
on Rabbit Hill.

Little Rabbit is _____
for grass to eat.

run	running

Away goes Little Rabbit.

He is _____ home.

Run, rabbit, _____!

Kitty Cat and Fat Cat

<table>
<tr><td>

About the story

Kitty Cat and Fat Cat are now becoming familiar characters. Kitty Cat's playful antics annoy Fat Cat who reacts in a typical way. This story supports the children's predictions.

</td><td>

Linking with other PM books

Kitty Cat	PM Plus Level 3
Kitty Cat and the Fish	PM Plus Level 5
My little cat	PM Plus Level 2

</td></tr>
</table>

Creating the atmosphere

Reread *Kitty Cat* and *Kitty Cat and the Fish* (Levels 3 and 5). Discuss the illustrations of both Kitty Cat and Fat Cat. Talk about their different features. Ask the children to draw pictures of each character on folded A2 sized paper. The children can use their books to write a label for each cat.

Focusing on the story

- **Cover** Read the title and talk about the illustration.
- **Pages 2–7** Encourage the children to use picture clues to predict the text. After reading page 7, many children will be able to anticipate what will happen next. Encourage this skill.
- **Pages 8–11** Demonstrate how to read these pages with intonation in order to express the meaning of the text.
- **Pages 12–15** Talk about the reactions of both cats. Encourage the children to reflect these by reading the text with the appropriate intonation. Ensure that they pause at the line spaces.
- **Page 16** Discuss why Fat Cat is unable to follow Kitty Cat in the little door.

Going beyond the story

- Ask the children to find the part in the story that they liked best. Have them draw a picture to illustrate this section and then share their illustrations with the class. The children could also read the appropriate text from the book or write their own story.

- Using play dough or clay, have the children make models of Kitty Cat and Fat Cat. Add labels describing their features or personalities.

Kitty Cat is a naughty little cat.

<table>
<tr><td>

Developing specific skills

- Talk about the endings: look*ing*, look*ed*
- Encourage reasoning and prediction. Ask, 'Why do you think …?'
- Reinforce directionality and the return sweep of longer sentences.

</td><td>

Using the blackline master

- Talk about the opposites 'up' and 'down'. Read each sentence and have the children write in the correct word.
- Discuss the illustrations of the slide. Predict and then write the words to go in each box. Ask the children to draw themselves in each picture.

</td></tr>
</table>

My name is _____

| up | down |

Fat Cat looked _____
at Kitty Cat.

Fat Cat's tail
went _____ and _____.

Kitty Cat ran
_____ to Fat Cat's tail.

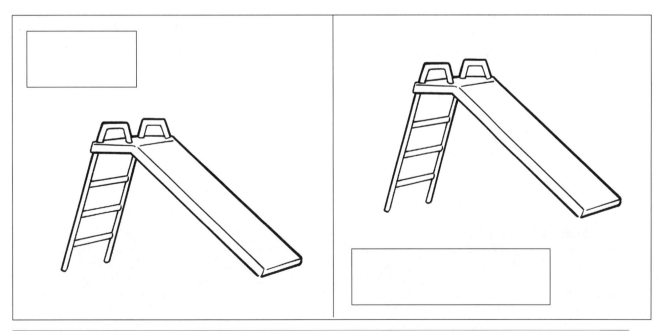

Billy is Hiding

About the story

Jack's little brother Billy cannot be found when Mum wants to take the boys out. This family situation will be familiar to many children.

Linking with other PM books

Jack and Billy series	PM Plus Levels 3 and 4
Hide and seek	PM Library Red Level
Where is Hannah?	PM Library Red Level

Creating the atmosphere

Play the game 'Hide and Seek'. Talk about the places where the children hid. Encourage them to explain why some places were better than others.

Focusing on the story

- **Cover** Talk about Mum and Jack's actions, then read the title with the children. Read the title again on the title page.

- **Pages 2–3** Read the text with the children. Talk about Mum's car keys and Mum's shopping bag. Ask, 'Where do you think Mum is going?'

- **Pages 4–5** Ask, 'Why didn't Billy come when Mum called?'

- **Pages 6–13** Have the children verbalise where Mum and Billy searched before reading the text. Ask, 'Do you think Billy is playing a game?'

- **Pages 14–15** Read Mum's remark in a joking voice so that the children understand its intent.

- **Page 16** Observe the children as they decode and respond to Billy's words. Ask, 'Does Billy think he has played a joke on Mum and Jack?'

Going beyond the story

- Revisit the illustrations. Make a list of all the places that Mum and Jack looked for Billy. Add pictures.

- Hide a familiar item of classroom equipment. Play a guessing game. One child asks, 'Where do you think I have hidden the _____?' The others in the group respond by saying, 'I think you have hidden the _____ in _____.'

Developing specific skills

- Question mark — talk about the punctuation symbol, name and meaning.
- Encourage reasoning and prediction. Ask, 'Why do you think …?'
- Revise the upper-case letters: J, B, M, L, H, W.

Using the blackline master

- Read the words 'here' and 'where' with the children. Explain how to write each word.
- Read the sentences before writing in the words.
- Read the last sentence. Talk about the importance of drawing a picture that matches the text.

My name is _____

here   here

Mum said,
"Come _____, Jack.
Come _____, Billy."

Where

Mum said,
"We are going in the car.
_____ is Billy?"

Mum and Jack
looked and looked
for Billy.

The Toytown Helicopter

About the story
This is the first in a series of fantasy stories about the Toytown vehicles.
In this story, the helicopter is late home because of heavy rain and the other vehicles are worried.

Linking with other PM books
Little Bulldozer	PM Library Yellow Level
Little Bulldozer helps again	PM Library Yellow Level
Down by the station	PM Library Readalongs

Creating the atmosphere
Read *Little Bulldozer* and *Little Bulldozer helps again* (PM Library Yellow Level) to the children, examining the concept of animated vehicles. Discuss the stylised vehicles in these two books.

Focusing on the story
- **Cover** Look at the features of the helicopter and compare them with those of a real helicopter.
- **Pages 2–3** Study the picture of the Toytown Garage. Discuss its purpose. Predict who might live in the garage. Observe and talk about the dark clouds behind the garage.
- **Pages 4–7** Talk about the vehicles that have returned to the garage. Discuss the concerned looks on their faces. Ask, 'Why do you think the vehicles look so worried?'
- **Pages 8–13** Discuss the heavy rain and the vehicles' concern for the helicopter's safety.

- **Pages 14–16** Look at the change in the weather. Have the children predict the happy ending.

Going beyond the story
- Have the children predict the conversation that may have taken place after page 16. Assist them in this imaginative situation to invent further dialogue between the vehicles.
- Invite the children to make finger puppets or cardboard cut-outs of each vehicle. Have them present a puppet show using both the text from the book and their own dialogue.

Developing specific skills
- Ensure correct directionality on double-page spreads.
- Recognise the initial letter and its associated word: h — helicopter, b — bus, t — tow truck.
- Notice the verb ending: ing — com*ing*.

Using the blackline master
- Read the names of each vehicle on the walls of the garage and the hangar.
- Ask the children to draw a small picture of each vehicle in its labelled place in the illustration.
- Demonstrate how to trace over and complete the word 'comes'.

My name is _____

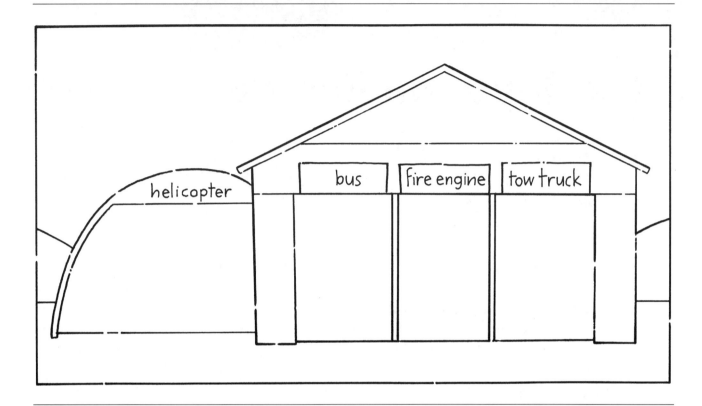

comes   comes   comes   _____

Here _____ the bus.

Here _____ the tow truck.

Here _____ the fire engine.

Here _____ the helicopter.

The Toytown Rescue

About the story

This is the second story in the PM Plus series about the Toytown vehicles. In this book, the bus has run off the road and is unable to move. The helicopter and the tow truck come to its rescue.

Linking with other PM books

The Toytown Helicopter	PM Plus Level 5
The bus song	PM Library Readalongs
Tim's favourite toy	PM Library Blue Level

Creating the atmosphere

Reread *The Toytown Helicopter* (Level 5). Discuss and list the kind of tasks that these Toytown vehicles might carry out. Have the children talk about their own toy vehicles.

Focusing on the story

- **Cover** Observe the vehicles and discuss the setting. Talk about the situation that may have preceded this picture. Read the title with the children both on the cover and the title page.

- **Pages 2–3** Study the vehicles' expressions. Discuss how the helicopter is feeling compared with the other two vehicles.

- **Pages 4–7** Talk about how the fire engine and the tow truck have reacted to the helicopter's news.

- **Pages 8–11** Discuss why the helicopter can see the bus and the tow truck cannot.

- **Pages 12–16** Have the children predict how the rescue will proceed.

Going beyond the story

- Invite the children to present a play based on the story. They could follow the text or improvise dialogue for each character.

- Have a special 'Toys' Day' at school (see *Tim's favourite toy*, PM Library Blue Level) where the children bring toy vehicles from home and talk about them to the rest of the class. The curriculum areas of oral and written language, and reading can be part of this exercise. Simple captions may be prepared at home or written at school and displayed with the toys.

Developing specific skills

- Reinforce directionality and return sweep on double-page spreads and longer sentences.
- Question mark — talk about the punctuation symbol, name and meaning.
- Understand the concept of first and last words.

Using the blackline master

- Demonstrate how to trace over and complete the word 'down'.
- Discuss the scene in the illustration. Predict where each vehicle might be placed.
- Read each sentence and confirm the predictions. Ask the children to draw the vehicles in their correct place.

My name is _____

down   down   down   _____

The bus is _____
in the grass.

The helicopter went
_____ to see the bus.

The tow truck went
_____ to the bus.

Sam's Picnic

About the story

Sam, Mum and Bingo go on a picnic. Unfortunately, their enjoyable outing is spoilt by an unexpected rain cloud.

Linking with other PM books

Sam and Bingo series	PM Plus Levels 3–5
r, p, c, h	PM Library Alphabet Starters
Teddy Bears' Picnic	PM Plus Level 3

Creating the atmosphere

Reread *Teddy Bears' Picnic* (Level 3). Encourage the children to talk about picnics that they have been to. Record some of these experiences on strips of card for the children to illustrate later, e.g. 'Callum went to the park for a picnic', 'Zoe went to the beach for a picnic.'

Focusing on the story

• **Cover** Many children will recognise Sam, her mother and Bingo from previous stories. Talk about the setting, the rug and the picnic basket. Read the title together on the cover and again on the title page.

• **Pages 2–3** Read the text with the children allowing them to use their decoding skills to attempt the words 'river' and 'picnic'.

• **Pages 4–5** Talk about the actions of Sam and her mother, and the fact they have not seen the large black clouds.

• **Pages 6–9** Write the words 'clouds' and 'rain' on the whiteboard. Explain in simple terms where rain comes from. Discuss Sam and Mum's actions.

• **Pages 10–11** Sam's disappointed face at the window will help the children to read the text with the appropriate expression.

• **Pages 12–13** Ask, 'How do you think Sam would be feeling?' Write the children's responses on the whiteboard.

• **Pages 14–16** Talk about the fun ending to the day.

Going beyond the story

• Make a large picnic basket from a cardboard box. Have the children paint the outside of the box and fill it with small containers or shapes cut from light card to represent picnic food and utensils.

Developing specific skills

• Reinforce directionality and the return sweep of longer sentences.
• Revisit letter names and sounds: b, w, r, p, c, h.
• Speech marks — talk about the punctuation symbol, name and meaning.

Using the blackline master

• Use r, p, c and h (PM Library Alphabet Starters) to reinforce each letter's sound and shape.
• Say the name of each picture and write its initial letter.
• Read and complete the sentences with the children.

My name is _____

r	p	c	h

  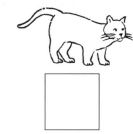 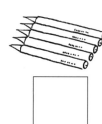

  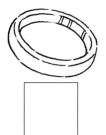 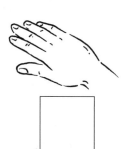

went	went

Sam and Mum and Bingo

_____ down

to the river.

Sam and Mum and Bingo

_____ home in the car.

RECOUNT

Running words: 35

The purpose of a recount is to retell the details of an event in sequential order. Letters and diaries are common forms of recounts. A recount is more personal than a report.

At the Toyshop

About the book

A little boy is staying with his Gran. They have been shopping together. Now he is writing a letter to his parents telling them about the exciting events of the day.

Linking with other PM books

The toy box	PM Plus Level 2
Jack's Birthday	PM Plus Level 4
Monkey on the Roof	PM Plus Level 5

Creating the atmosphere

Have the children recall any shopping excursions with their grandparents. List these events using simple sentence structures, e.g. 'We had lunch in the big mall. We went to the supermarket.'

Focusing on the book

- **Cover** Read the title to the children. Encourage them to study the photograph and predict what is happening. Read the title again on the title page.

- **Pages 2–3** Read the text and confirm the children's predictions. Read the child's own letter on page 4. Ensure that the children understand how these two pages and subsequent pages work together.

- **Pages 4–5** Help the children to understand that the little boy is now recalling the events of the day.

- **Pages 6–11** Talk about the choice that the little boy will have to make. Ask, 'Which toy do you think he will choose?' Continue to read the child's own writing to reinforce the meaning of the text.

- **Pages 12–15** Ask, 'Why do you think he chose the dinosaur? How do you think Gran feels about his choice?'

- **Page 16** Read the letter without interruption.

Going beyond the book

- Write each sentence on separate cards keeping the text layout exactly as it is written in the book. In pairs or in small groups, ask the children to reassemble the letter in the correct order of events.

> We went to the toyshop.

> We looked at the dinosaur.

- Using the cards from the previous activity, have the children draw a picture to match each sentence. These pictures could then be pasted into an enlarged book. Using thick black felt pens, copy the matching sentence under each picture. Talk about the importance of the illustration matching the text.

Developing specific skills

- Talk about the layout of a letter.
- Discuss the final sound in: looked, liked.
- Notice the full stop at the end of each sentence.

Using the blackline master

- Reread the letter on page 16 of the book.
- Read the letter on the blackline master and recall the missing sentences.
- Encourage the children to use the photograph of the dinosaur on page 16 of the book as a model for their illustration.

My name is _____

Dear Mum and Dad,

We went to the toyshop.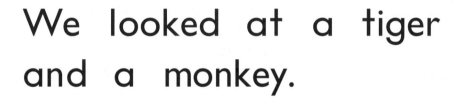

We looked at the dinosaur.

_____

We looked at a tiger
and a monkey.

_____

Here is my dinosaur.

_____ from

Nick

EXPLANATORY | The purpose of an explanation is to define an idea or to explain cause and effect, e.g. 'What is play? Why do puddles disappear?'

Running words: 80

Time for Play

About the book
This explanatory text reflects the variety of activities that children can do as they play.

Linking with other PM books
We dress up	PM Plus Level 1
Sam's Race	PM Plus Level 4
My Tower	PM Plus Level 4
Hide and seek	PM Library Red Level

Creating the atmosphere
Reread the PM Library and PM Plus Story Books linked to the theme 'Time for Play'. List the play activities featured in these books on a chart for the children to illustrate and to refer to as they read *Time for Play*.

Focusing on the book
- **Cover** Read the title to the children and ask them to give their ideas about the content. Talk about the details in the photographs.

- **Pages 2–16** Study each photograph carefully and discuss the children's actions before reading the text.

- **Page 2** Give the children time to explain why the text says, 'We love playing.'

- **Pages 6–7** Talk about the game 'Hide and Seek'. Have the children describe in sequential order the rules of the game.

- **Pages 8–9** Ask, 'Why do you think the children are running races on the grass?'

- **Pages 12–13** Ask the children to explain the best way to build a tower using blocks.

- **Page 16** Refer back to the text on page 2. Ask, 'Why do you think the same sentence was written on pages 2 and 16?'

Going beyond the book
- Revisit the play activities in *Time for Play*. Have the children suggest other play activities that they enjoy. Record these on the chart (see 'Creating the atmosphere'). Using these additional ideas, make up the text for another book. Begin the new book with the same statement, 'We love playing.'

- Read the book again and discuss whether it would be possible to do some or all of these play activities at school. If possible, have the children organise some of these activities under teacher supervision. When the children have completed the activities, have them draw and write a brief explanation about the activity that they enjoyed the most.

Developing specific skills
- Introduce the structure of a sentence.
- Revise capital letters and full stops.
- Reinforce directionality on double-page spreads.

Using the blackline master
- Read each sentence starter to the children.
- Discuss the different activities that they do at each of these times. List the children's ideas on a chart and have them use it as a reference when completing the blackline master.
- Reinforce the importance of details in illustrations.

My name is _____ PM⁺

At lunchtime,

I _____

_____ .

At hometime,

I _____

_____ .

At bedtime,

I _____

_____ .

REPORT	A report describes a topic and is usually written in the present tense. It is an impersonal statement of fact, and may include observation.

Running words: 94

Playing with Dough

About the book

This book portrays an oral sharing situation. Children show and tell the activities that they have just completed to their teacher and peers.

Linking with other PM books

In the garden   PM Plus Level 1
Time for Play   PM Plus Non-fiction Levels 5 and 6
We dress up   PM Plus Level 1

Creating the atmosphere

Show the children how to make rolls and balls from play dough. Give them time to experiment before they discuss their work.

Focusing on the book

- **Cover** Look carefully at the actions of the children. Talk about the play dough. Read the title together. Encourage the children to read the title on the title page without assistance.

- **Pages 2–3** Relate the scene to similar situations in the children's own classroom. Discuss what the girl has made from dough. Encourage the children to use the initial letter as a clue.

- **Pages 4–13** Discuss each photograph and vignette with the children before they attempt to read the text independently. Observe their retention of high frequency words, and their use of context and initial letters to decode interest words.

- **Pages 14–15** Have available some plastic shapes that are similar to the ones on page 14. Write the word 'shapes' on the whiteboard. Discuss the 'sh' sound in relation to the word 'shouted'.

- **Page 16** Match the word 'Ben' in the text with the play dough 'Ben' made by the boy.

Going beyond the book

- Talk about the different things that were made from dough in the book. Have the children copy these examples or make their own. Encourage them to write their own descriptive captions paying attention to the upper-case letters and full stops.

- Use play dough to make teddy bear shapes. Press the finished shape firmly onto a piece of cardboard. When the dough surface is dry to touch, paint it with acrylic paint. Staple the finished artwork to a wall display on the same day in order to avoid the cardboard curling as the dough dries. Add captions.

Developing specific skills

- Assist the children to understand the concept of a sentence.
- Question mark — reinforce the understanding of the punctuation symbol, name and meaning.
- Revise upper-case letters.

Using the blackline master

- Have the children read each sentence starter on the blackline master.
- Explain that they will be making things from dough. They will then finish writing each sentence and draw a picture of the item.

My name is _____

Here is a _____.

Look _____

_____.

Here are some

_____.

Look _____

_____.

This is _____.

Can you see

_____

_____?

EXPOSITORY

Running words: 103

An exposition presents an argument or states a firmly held position. Persuasive language is used to justify a point of view, with reasoning.

Where is it Safe to Play?

About the book

This text provides opportunities for children to think, reason and give their opinion about safe places to play.

Linking with other PM books

Tiger, Tiger	PM Library Red Level
Little Chimp Runs Away	PM Plus Level 6
Baby Hippo	PM Library Yellow Level
Tiny and the big wave	PM Library Yellow Level

Creating the atmosphere

Discuss the word 'safe' with the children to find out their understanding of the concept and how it affects them personally. Accept all ideas and write them on a chart to read back to the children. Encourage further discussion.

Focusing on the book

- **Cover** Read the title to the children pausing for them to respond. Study the photographs on the cover and the vignette on the title page.

- **Pages 2–3** Have the children share any first-hand experiences of younger family members and keeping them safe.

- **Pages 4–7** Talk about fences. Relate the concept to the baby's playpen on the previous page. Discuss why it is important for swimming pools to be fenced.

- **Pages 8–9** Ask, 'Why is it safe to play at school?' Study the photograph and list some of the reasons why school is a safe place to play.

- **Pages 10–13** Talk about road traffic. Before turning the page, discuss possible solutions to the text question on page 13.

- **Pages 14–16** Encourage the sharing of ideas.

Going beyond the book

- Make an enlarged book about situations where the children feel safe. Record a question with the text. Add illustrations. Use this book often for additional reading and as a discussion starter.

- Establish three rules for the classroom that would help to keep the children safe. Write these rules on a large chart for the children to decorate.

- Fold a long strip of paper concertina style. Cut it into the shape of a person. Open the paper to show a row of people holding hands. Ask the children to give situations when it is a good idea to hold hands in order to keep safe, e.g. 'A big person should hold our hand when we cross the road.'

Developing specific skills

- Discuss the text and photographic layout.
- Clarify understanding of questions and answers.
- Reinforce the integration of meaning, structure and visual cues.

Using the blackline master

- Using the book, list safe places to play.
- Have the children suggest other safe places.
- Encourage the children to write a qualifying sentence for each of the two places that they chose, e.g. 'I am playing in my back yard.' Have them add illustrations.

My name is _____

Baby can play here.
Baby is safe.

I can play here.
I am safe.

I can play here.
I am safe.

Blackline master 34 • *Where is it Safe to Play?* © Nelson, 2000.

This page may be photocopied for educational use within the purchasing institution.

PM Plus Teachers' Guide: Levels 3–5   101

A procedural text gives sequential instructions about how to make or do something.

Running words: 121

Making a Cat and a Mouse

About the book
This procedural text has been separated into two parts giving clear instructions for making a cat and a mouse. The simple instructions, the vignettes and the colour-coded pages support the high frequency words.

Linking with other PM books
Making a rabbit	PM Plus Non-fiction Level 1
Making a bird	PM Plus Non-fiction Level 1
Making a dinosaur	PM Plus Non-fiction Level 1
Cat and Mouse	PM Library Starters Two

Creating the atmosphere
Provide the children with copies of *Making a rabbit*, *Making a bird* and *Making a dinosaur*. (PM Plus Level 1). Have them read through the books and select an animal to make. Emphasise the importance of reading the text and following a procedure.

Focusing on the book
• **Cover** Read the title together and study the details of the models carefully. Draw the children's attention to the colour-coded paper.

• **Pages 2–3** Comment on the vignette at the top of the double-page spread. Talk about the different sizes of paper for the body, head and tail. Encourage the children to use the vignettes and initial letters to decode the unknown words.

• **Pages 4–9** Discuss the sequence of vignettes on each double-page spread. Demonstrate the procedure after the text has been read.

• **Pages 10–16** Encourage the children to recognise similarities and differences between these pages and pages 2–9. Talk about the list of materials on pages 10

and 11. Demonstrate the procedure after the text has been read.

Going beyond the book
• After reading the text, have the children follow the procedure carefully and make a cat and a mouse each.

• Have the children draw lines and curves on firm paper. They can then cut out and paste these shaped pieces of paper onto a coloured background to make patterns.

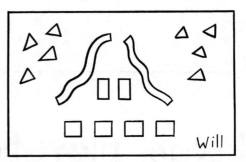

• Photocopy the outline of a body shape onto light-weight card. Have the children cut these shapes out and 'dress' them with collage materials. Display these 'children' attractively on a background showing a school or playground scene.

Developing specific skills
• Ensure correct directionality for this text form.
• Reinforce reading to follow instructions.
• Encourage recall of high frequency words.

Using the blackline master
• Explain the vignettes showing the materials needed and how the puppets are attached to the finger.
• Read each sentence and talk about the different markings for each animal.
• Demonstrate how to decorate and make a finger puppet.

My name is _____

Finger puppets

You will need:

  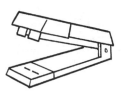

 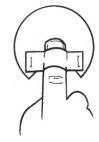

front   back

Here is a tiger.

Here is a bear.

Here is a monkey.

| VERSE | Verse is rhythmic language that pleases the ear and stimulates the mind. |

Toys and Play

About the book
This book has many small verses for children to recite individually or in small groups. Common play situations and the rhythmical patterns of the language will assist children to decode unknown words.

Linking with other PM books
Sam and Bingo	PM Plus Level 3
Kitty Cat	PM Plus Level 3
Jack's Birthday	PM Plus Level 4
Ben's teddy bear	PM Library Red Level

Creating the atmosphere
Reread PM Library and PM Plus Story Books linked to the theme 'Toys and Play'. Discuss the toys and the play activities in each story.

Focusing on the book
The verses could be studied over a period of several days.
- **Cover** Read the title to the children and discuss the illustrations.
- **Pages 2–16** Discuss each illustration. Encourage the children to share their own experiences about toys and play as they find an illustration of personal interest. Read each verse twice to the children. Have the children read each verse aloud, as a group. Observe the children as they read the verses independently. Provide any individual support that may be required.

Going beyond the book
- Ask the children to select their favourite verse from the book to learn from memory. Have them paint a picture to go with their selected verse. Invite another class to listen to the verses as they are recited.
- Have the children make collage pictures of themselves to attach to a mural of a playground. Paste enlarged copies of each verse to the mural for use as an additional reading activity.

Developing specific skills
- Explain that verse has a different text layout.
- Listen to the sounds that rhyme.
- Encourage the use of initial letter and picture match to decode unknown words.

Using the blackline master
- Read the verse together.
- Encourage the children to predict the missing words from the context.
- Find the verse in the book and read it again, together.
- Write in the missing words.

My name is _____

Let's go . . .

Up the net
and _____ the pole,
in the tunnel
and _____ the hole.

Back _____ the tunnel
and out the side . . .
_____ the ladder
and down the slide.

| Up | down | in | out |

Language monitoring check

Levels 3, 4 and 5
Skills, understandings and behaviours

Date

Speaking and listening

Listens to stories								
Tells stories based on own experiences								
Explains about own pictures								
Controls a range of appropriate oral vocabulary to suit the situation								

Reading and writing

Has one-to-one correspondence								
Demonstrates correct directional movement with text								
Is linking the text to the meaning								
Has retained many high frequency words								
Demonstrates front and back of book								
Is developing a memory for text								
Is linking picture clues to text								
Talks to others about own stories and pictures								
Reads back own stories								
Is beginning to link sounds to letter symbols								
Is attempting unknown words in own reading and writing using the initial letter								

Viewing and presenting

Observes more detail in illustrations								

General comments (date all observations):

Reading record

Name: _____ **Age:** _____ **Date:** _____

Text: *Sam's Balloon* _____ **Level:** *3* _____ **Running words:** *54* _____

Summary: _____

_____

_____

Page		E	SC	Errors MSV	Self corrections MSV
3	Here comes a clown.				
	Look at the balloons.				
5	Sam said,				
	"Mum! Look at the balloons."				
7	Sam said,				
	"Mum! Look at the balloons.				
	Come on!"				
9	**"No balloons?"** said Sam.				
11	"Here is a balloon,"				
	said the clown.				
13	"Look at the clown,"				
	said Mum.				
15	"Look at the **balloon!**"				
	said Sam.				
16	"My balloon is a dog,"				
	said Sam.				
	Totals				

Reading record

Name: _____   **Age:** _____   **Date:** _____

Text: _Mother Bird_____   **Level:** _4_____   **Running words:** _____ _75_

Summary: _____

_____

_____

Page		E	SC	Errors MSV	Self corrections MSV
3	Mother Bird is looking for a worm.				
5	Up in the tree,				
	the baby birds are hungry.				
7	Mother Bird looks and looks				
	for a worm.				
9	Here comes a worm.				
	Mother Bird sees the worm.				
10	Here comes a cat.				
	The cat sees Mother Bird.				
13	Mother Bird sees the cat.				
	Up goes Mother Bird.				
15	Up, up, up, goes Mother Bird.				
	Mother Bird goes up				
	to the baby birds in the tree.				
16	The worm is for the baby birds.				
	Totals				

Reading record

Name: _____ **Age:** _____ **Date:** _____

Text: _The Toytown Rescue_ **Level:** _5_ **Running words:** _100_

Summary: _____

_____

_____

Page		E	SC	Errors MSV	Self corrections MSV
2	Here comes the Toytown helicopter.				
4	"The bus is down in the grass!"				
	said the helicopter to the tow truck.				
	"Come on!"				
6	Away went the tow truck.				
7	Away went the helicopter.				
8	"I can not see the bus,"				
	said the tow truck to the helicopter.				
10	"I can see the bus," said the helicopter.				
	"Come down to the big tree."				
12	The tow truck went down				
	to the big tree.				
	"I can see the bus!" said the tow truck.				
	"Good," said the helicopter.				
14	"Oh, I am happy to see you,"				
	said the bus.				
	"Come on," said the tow truck.				
16	"Come home to the garage."				
	Totals				

Reading record

Name: _____   **Age:** _____   **Date:** _____

Text: _At the Toyshop_ _____   **Levels:** _5&6_ _____   **Running words:** _35_ _____

Summary: _____

_____

_____

Page		E	SC	Errors MSV	Self corrections MSV
2	Dear Mum and Dad,				
4	We went to the toyshop.				
6	We looked at the dinosaur.				
8	We looked at the cars.				
10	We looked at a tiger				
	and a monkey.				
12	I liked the dinosaur.				
14	Here is my dinosaur.				
	Totals				

Reading record

Name: _____ Age: _____ Date: _____

Text: _____ Level: _____ Running words: _____

Summary: _____

_____

_____

Page		E	SC	Errors MSV	Self corrections MSV
	Totals				

PM Plus titles Levels 1–8

LEVEL 1

I am running
Baby
In the garden
The play
We dress up
In our classroom
Up in the sky
Going on holiday
Look at the house
Balloons

LEVEL 1

Non-fiction
Making a rabbit
Making a dinosaur
Making a bird

LEVEL 2

My little cat
My clothes
Big and little
Big sea animals
The toy box
My sandcastle
Going out
Playing outside
Party hats
The parade

LEVEL 2

Non-fiction
Up and down
Round and round
On and off

LEVEL 3

Story Books
Photo Time
Kitty Cat
Sam and Bingo
Little Chimp
Here Comes Little Chimp
Jack and Billy
Sam's Balloon
Baby Wakes Up
The Big Hill
Teddy Bears' Picnic

LEVEL 4

Story Books
My Tower
My Book
Little Chimp and Big Chimp
Sam's Race
Jack's Birthday
Bedtime
The Lucky Dip
Let's Pretend
Red Puppy
Mother Bird

LEVEL 5

Story Books
Kitty Cat and the Fish
Bingo's Ice Cream
Baby Panda
Monkey on the Roof
Run, Rabbit, Run!
Kitty Cat and Fat Cat
Billy is Hiding
The Toytown Helicopter
The Toytown Rescue
Sam's Picnic

LEVELS & 5 & 6

Non-fiction
At the Toyshop
Time for Play
Playing with Dough
Where is it Safe to Play?
Making a Cat and a Mouse
Toys and Play

LEVEL 6

Story Books
The Toytown Fire Engine
Little Chimp Runs Away
Billy Can Count
Clever Fox
Sam and the Waves
Speedy Bee
Here Come the Shapes
Bread for the Ducks
Walk, Ride, Run
The Big Hit

LEVEL 7

Story Books
Sam Goes to School
Mother's Day
Bingo's Birthday
New Boots
Red Squirrel Hides Some Nuts
The Leaf Boats
Dilly Duck and Dally Duck
A Crocodile and a Whale
Jolly Roger and the Treasure
The Big Yellow Castle

LEVEL 8

Story Books
Kitty Cat Plays Inside
A Party for Brown Mouse
Katie's Caterpillar
Max Rides His Bike
Max Goes Fishing
Jumbo
Look Out for Bingo
The Little White Hen
Roar Like a Tiger
Max and the Little Plant

LEVELS & 8 & 9

Non-fiction
It is Raining
Hot Sunny Days
Rain is Water
Where Did All the Water Go?
Making a Caterpillar
The Sun, the Wind and the Rain